TOP DOWN
— FOR —
TODDLERS

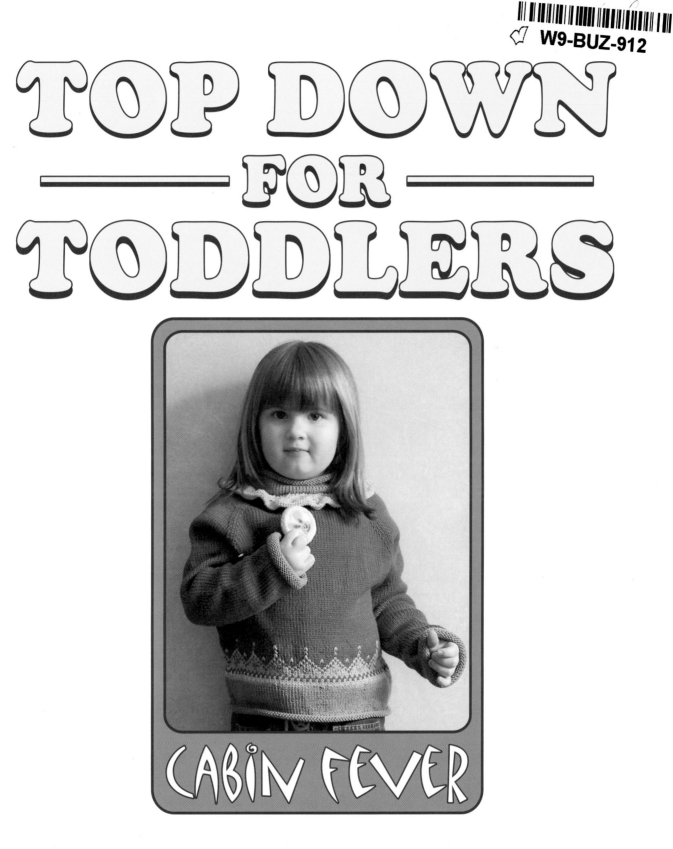

CABIN FEVER

Thanks Mom, Thanks Dad.

Copy editor: Judith Small
Cover design: John Emberson
Illustrations: John Emberson
Layout and design: Lynda Gemmell
Pattern checkers: Mary K. Hobbs and Gayle Bunn
Photography: Mary Bray
Technical editor: Deb Gemmell
Project management: And So Forth Press

http://www.cabinfever.ca

email: info@cabinfever.ca

ISBN 0-9735657-0-5

Printed in Canada.

ACKNOWLEDGEMENTS

There are always an amazing number of people involved in the production of a book, along with those lending support along the way.

We would like to thank our insightful and encouraging test knitters as they knit and re-knit: Leith Clarke, Bernice Vollick, Elizabeth Gowen, Sophy Cooper, and Dana Gibbons, who is also one of our designers. Paul Court (Deb's husband) for his encouragement and support; Sophy Cooper for cheerfully keeping the orders rolling out the door while we ripped our hair out; our sister Heather for listening while we went on endlessly about the book; our good friend and editor Judith Small who succumbed to the lure of knitting (after many years away) after reading so many knitting books to get herself up to speed. And to Mary Bray, another friend, knitter, and our photogra- pher, who took and re-took shots of sweaters in the midst of selling her house.

Mary K. Hobbs worked all hours of the night and weekends to get the patterns checked - even with the enticing distraction of her brand new grandchild, Tyler.

John Emberson, our graphic artist, and Jim Thomson from Rose Printing, were the only non-knitters actively involved in the book, but they took great interest, were supportive, and learned how to say things like "stitch definition" so convincingly it almost seemed they knew what they were talking about.

And lastly, to our customers, for their support and their inspiring requests for "more, more, more!"

TABLE OF CONTENTS

Introduction 4

Our Design Philosophy 4

A Story of Two Sisters 6

Friends of Cabin Fever 7

An Overview 8

The Language of Knitting 13

Increases 16

The Basic Pullover 18

The Basic Cardigan 23

The Basic Hat 28

Jazz It Up! 29

The Basic Sock 31

The Russian Hat 33

Little Viking 34

Puffy Stripes 39

Megan's Ruffle 46

Dancing Princess 52

The Poncho 58

The PaintBox 60

Classic Cable 62

Sweatshirt Style 69

Woven Ridges 74

Florabel 79

Carnival Coat 84

Texture Time 90

Calypso Jacket 95

Technical Bits 101

Other Reading 103

Supply Sources 103

Index 104

INTRODUCTION

Welcome to the latest creative product from Cabin Fever. We're especially proud of this book, as it showcases the work of our Cabin Fever designers. It is also intended to introduce you to the fabulous world of knitting from the top down.

Why are we so taken with the concept of top-down knitting? First, because it fits so beautifully with our design approach: knitting with minimal finishing, and no sewing! By using circular needles and working the project in one piece, there are no pieces to sew together after the knitting is finished. After you cast off the bottom edge, your garment is ready to wear.

To introduce you to the talents of our six Cabin Fever designers, we designed, sized and tested a set of basic top-down patterns: pullover, cardigan, a hat and a pair of socks. Then we gave each of the Friends of Cabin Fever free rein to let their creative ideas run wild!

The results are easy to do and fast to knit; ideal for relatively new knitters and those who've never explored top-down techniques. Some are basic and practical for new Moms (but always jazzed up with a little extra designer touch), and some have fun and funky approaches to entice Grandmas and little ones alike with textures, colours and bobbles.

So please enjoy, and we hope that this book entices you to try a whole new way to knit. If you've already knit from the top down then please sit back, enjoy the designs, and maybe create an interpretation of your own!

Deb and Lynda Gemmell

Note: Dana created a hat (see right) for the Calypso Jacket. The free hat pattern can be found on our web page:

http://www.cabinfever.ca

OUR DESIGN PHILOSOPHY

Simply put, we're nuts about knitting, but not about the dreaded sewing-up that has traditionally come after the knitting is done.

So, our overall knitting philosophy is simple. We believe that, within reason, when you finish knitting and have worked that final cast off, you're finished! We don't want to sew seams, or wrestle in sleeves that don't seem to fit into armholes. We don't like to feel that the knitting is just a small part of creating a finished garment.

We're knitters and we love to knit but neither one of us likes to sew. It just makes us cranky!

We believe that when you are finished the knitting — you're finished the garment!

The majority of our designs are knit in one piece, from the bottom up or from the top down. Others are knit in a modular fashion, but again with little or no sewing. As we go to press only two of our several dozen patterns have seams to sew!

Minimal finishing means looking for innovative methods to reduce or eliminate the amount of sewing needed to achieve an attractive finished garment. Knitting in the round with circular needles lends itself to this approach. And knitting from the top, starting with the collar and working down to the bottom edge, means no sewing whatsoever. Perfect!

And so, the beginning of the idea for this book.

A Story of Two Sisters

Cabin Fever is the business created by us, sisters Deb and Lynda Gemmell, to feed our knitting habit. From an idea hatched on the deck of our Northern Ontario cabin over several summers, Cabin Fever has grown into the largest independent hand-knitting pattern publisher in Canada.

With Deb as the knitting technical expert and Lynda contributing the business and computer know-how, we launched Cabin Fever in 1997.

We began with a tiny retail shop so "cosy" that we could not have more than one customer and one of us in the place at the same time.

But much as we enjoy working with knitters who happen to be customers, our real passion was not running a retail store. We had a much greater interest in producing and publishing our own designs.

So, Cabin Fever the design company was born. Our first hat pattern was launched in 1998 and is still selling strongly.

During the exercise of writing our first patterns we also developed our own distinctive pattern writing style, which has continued to this day. Our patterns are longer than many, as we like to ensure that you know why you are doing a particular technique, as well as how.

The success of our initial patterns has lead us to concentrate our efforts into the production of new designs. Over time, it also lead us to the decision to broaden our designer base. But it wasn't a decision we made lightly!

Our concern was to ensure that when you pick up a Cabin Fever pattern you can make certain assumptions about the pattern and its structure: you will get a wearable garment with minimal finishing, simplicity in approach, and clear instructions with useful "chat" to keep you company as you progress.

Would we be able to continue to provide this level of service with new designers? Ultimately we decided we could, with care, and Friends of Cabin Fever was born.

We approached our friend Shirley Scott (aka Shirl the Purl) and in 2001 Shirl's first pattern was published. We now have more Canadian designers publishing under the Cabin Fever Friends' umbrella, and you'll find their work showcased in this book.

The making of this book was challenging, exciting and extremely rewarding. We hope you get as much pleasure from it as we have!

DEB GEMMELL

Deb started knitting from the top down when her own children were little tykes, for all the reasons that have kept this technique in her repertoire: easy length adjustment to accommodate growth spurts, knitting that's easy enough for a beginner since children's clothes don't have as many picky fitting issues, and of course no sewing up! Although she respects the time consuming and detailed work involved to sew up the pieces, Deb admits to having wardrobes of unfinished sweaters tucked away in closets due to her personal aversion to what has traditionally come after the knitting is finished.

What can we look forward to from Deb? Her project bags now include socks with a new cuff and toe technique, a poncho for a child (watch for different stitch patterns for the borders!), a dressy poncho with lace, and some wrist warmers for knitters and computer friends.

LYNDA GEMMELL

Although Lynda's travels have taken to her to over 18 countries, now it's more often her patterns for Cabin Fever that get to see the world. Those "What do we want to do?" conversations on the deck with her sister Deb launched Lynda out of the corporate sphere, and into a much more enjoyable career as designer, website wrangler, publisher, and creative entrepreneur. This could explain her fondness for designing hats - she wears so many!

When she's not knitting, thinking about knitting or writing or formatting knitting patterns you might find Lynda pursuing one of her other interests: working at her other business of book development, reading mystery stories in the bathtub, trying to stay upright behind a team of sled dogs, doting on her nieces and nephews, or spending time on the cross-trainer at the Y.

Deb and Lynda's designs have been published in the Knit Hats!, Knit Baby Heads & Toes!, Knit Christmas Stockings! hard cover series of books, all from Storey Publishing and in Donna Kooler's Encyclopedia of Knitting, Leisure Arts, 2004.

FRIENDS OF CABIN FEVER

DANA GIBBONS

We're inspired by Dana — a self-taught knitter who learned during her breaks while working as a nurse in an Infant Intensive Care Unit. Once she mastered stitch formation, she forged ahead. As her patterns (and beautifully-dressed granddaughters) demonstrate, Dana has never looked back.

Among the benefits of top-down knitting, Dana cites the ease of working this method in the places she often knits — while travelling, at sports events, or in waiting rooms — because it's easier to have all the pieces together and row counts correct.

Dana brings her experience as a mother of four to these projects, with practical touches like extra buttons for security, looser neck bands to accommodate kids' heads being larger in proportion to their bodies than adults', and buttonholes on both sides of the garment so it's equally wearable, whether handed down to a girl or boy.

SHIRL THE PURL

Shirley describes herself as a retired librarian who has had the great pleasure of knitting the days away for several years now. That joyous attitude about knitting is combined with an entirely practical approach to knitting for children! As one of four girls, Shirl remembers her mother struggling with tiny buttons, so she says that children's clothes should first be designed for easy on/off. She also knows how much parents appreciate clothes that will last more than one season.

Her dedication to designing strong and serviceable garments with a classic and casual style gives Shirl's creations an heirloom quality that we love. As Shirley says "I often find myself trying to recreate garments that I could buy ready made in stores. I suppose I am trying to reclaim authorship of these clothes...or confer on them the dignity and blessing of handwork...or goodness knows what."

Shirl is the author of *Canada Knits, Craft and Comfort in a Northern Land*, McGraw-Hill Ryerson, 1990. Shirl is also the founder and former editor of "Knitter's News".

MAUREEN MASON-JAMIESON

With a style that she describes as "quirky," Maureen adds another creative twist to our line-up of patterns for toddlers. As she says about the core patterns, "They give you a basic foundation for a design that you can turn into an individual garment."

In these patterns for Cabin Fever, Maureen has applied her own love for colours (and interesting combinations of colours), and her notion that children's clothes need to be comfortable and fun to wear for the child, while being interesting for the knitter to create. The results are undoubtedly fun!

Maureen continues to work with top-down techniques, and is currently creating a top-down evening jacket, as well as on a modular knit coat. Maureen has had designs published in the Knitter's and Interweave magazines. You can see more of Maureen's work, and read about the workshops she conducts at shows and guilds, at www.kinverknits.com.

MEGAN LACEY

A knitter from age 8, Megan has been designing her own patterns since 1996. Originally inspired by her grandmother's beautiful handknit sweaters, today Megan finds her ideas in the colours and patterns of nature; the simplicity of moss growing over an unusual shaped rock can be all it takes to spark the idea for a sweater.

When asked what advice she has for knitters, Megan says it's important to get the tension right; if you don't knit to the correct tension, you won't get the right size. She also believes that knitters should buy good quality yarn because after all the work put into making a sweater, it should be made in something that will last.

Megan knits mostly Nordic styles, and her designs tend to have Fair Isle patterns in them — a seemingly complex technique that Megan makes surprisingly simple to knit.

Megan has designs published in Knitter's Magazine and the *Socks,Socks,Socks* book by XRX, 1999.

ASSUMPTIONS

We make certain assumptions for the use of this book.

We assume that you can knit; that you have knit a scarf or two and know how to cast on, can work knit and purl stitches, and know how to cast off/bind off.

But don't be alarmed if you're not an experienced knitter! A number of the patterns you'll find here are intended for beginners, and are written for this audience.

If you've never knit in the round before, please don't hesitate to try it. It could change your knitting life!

AN OVERVIEW

KNITTING FROM THE TOP DOWN

Knitting from the top down fits perfectly with our criteria of minimal finishing. In our minds this is knitting heaven.

The pullover and cardigan are both knit in one piece. The pullover is knit in the round. The cardigan is worked back and forth on a circular needle, knitting the front, back, and second front all at once. A big, big bonus for knitting from the top down is that it's pretty much impossible to get much sewing in (even if you wanted to, and we don't!).

If you like knitting up various bits of a garment and then sewing it together, give this book to a good knitting buddy. The most sewing you'll be required to do will be sewing in the ends of your yarn, sewing on buttons (we've yet to find a solution to that one) and any fancy decorations you choose to use to jazz up the finished garment. No sewing in of sleeves, no attaching the back to the front--this is a book for knitters who love to knit.

Knitting from the top down is great for kids clothing

True or False?

TRUE.

Why? Well, there are several reasons:

You can try the "work in progress" on the wiggly little creature to make sure the sweater is the right size as you go.

It's always a good idea to knit items for the little ones just a bit big, as they seem to grow at an amazing rate. You can try the sweater on for the perfect sleeve length, although knitting the sleeves a little longer may be a good idea. Most cuffs can be rolled up for the first little while.

As they grow, toddlers tend to grow in length first, then width. Which brings us to another advantage: even after the sweater is finished and has been worn, you can extend the length of the cuffs and bottom edges to catch up with the growing wearer. Just unravel the cast-off edge, put the open stitches on a needle and knit a few more rounds.

It is helpful to plan ahead and put aside some of the yarn especially for this purpose. If you don't have any more of the exact same yarn, try taking off the cuffs and bottom edge and adding a different colour. Usually if you have a new colour in more than one place it looks like it was supposed to be there all along.

Pullovers for small children don't necessarily need a designated front or back (although it does help on a cardigan!). This is an enormous bonus during those "I can do it myself" years. A child cannot make a mistake and put these pullovers on backwards.

Aside: Knitting from the top down works very well for adults too but there are additional complications to dealing with the adult figure to achieve a comfortable fit. We are not recommending that you size these garments up to adult sizes but we do have a number of adult top-down patterns which you can see and order at our website:

http://www.cabinfever.ca

KNITTING IN THE ROUND

Most patterns that you are probably familiar with have you begin at the bottom edge of a sweater and knit UP the body until you arrive at the neck. It's just the way things have always been done, right?

Of course the majority of commercial patterns also suggest that you knit a front and a separate back. Oh, and while you're at it, have a separate sleeve...no, make that two. And then (horrors!) sew the whole shooting match together. It makes us tired and cranky just thinking about it, never mind actually doing it!

There's got to be a better way. And there is.

Knitting in the round means knitting the front, back and sleeves all at once, with your garment looking like a sweater from the beginning.

Knitting in the round is not a new concept, and has been widely used for centuries. Elizabeth Zimmermann rejuvenated this approach in North America during the 1970's with her many articles, books, videos and TV programs. Additionally, there is an excellent software program called The Sweater Wizard which you can use to design sweaters from the top down-- as well as in the round, side-to-side, flat etc. See supplies, at the end of the book.

Knitting in the round simply means using a circular needle, or double-pointed needles, and working the stitches in a continuous circle making a large tube of knitting, as shown in Photo 1.

Photo 1: *Working in the round creates a tube of continuous knitting. This hat (worked from the I-cord tip down to the brim) shows that the right side faces the knitter at all times.*

Generally speaking, most of the hundreds of knitters we've talked with prefer the "knit" stitch over the "purl" stitch. Knitting in the round lets knitters do only the knit stitch if they prefer. To achieve a stocking stitch item (hat, sweater, etc) you simply knit every round. No purling required.

Again, speaking in generalities, most knitters can work the knit stitch faster than the purl stitch and therefore, knitting in the round is often significantly faster than knitting flat. Because you are always working the same stitch you can achieve a beautifully even tension and smooth appearance.

Plus, you don't need to sew up the seams later which, for us, means the garments will actually get finished and worn instead of languishing in drawers or boxes as UFOs (unfinished objects) for years.

Many people refer to this construction as seamless knitting. This is quite correct as the knitting evolves as a tube without sewn side-seams.

Seamless knitting AND no sewing! Well, except for the buttons and the yarn ends--always read the fine print.

TECHNIQUES

The starting point to working in the round is the actual joining of the Cast On round to form your circular tube.

The Joining Round: Most patterns will say something like

> "Join in the round being careful not to twist your stitches".

After you have Cast On the requisite number of stitches, allow the circular needle to curve around to its natural shape, a circle. Take care to smooth all the stitches so the Cast On edge is pointing down, in the same direction, and are not twisted around the needle. See an example of twisted stitches below.

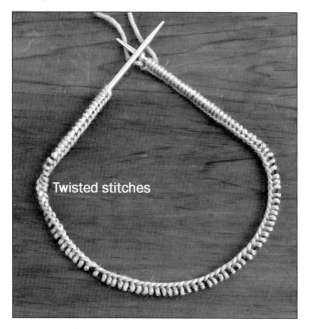

Twisted stitches

Photo 2: A long-tail Cast On with twisted stitches on the left-hand side of the needle.

The next example shows stitches sitting properly, all in the same direction:

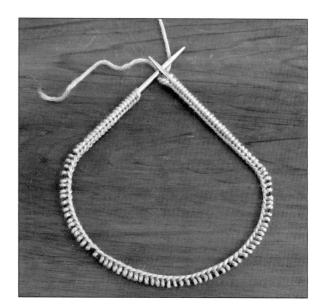

Photo 3: The same long-tail Cast On with all the stitches leaning in the same direction.

Once the stitches are all leaning in the same direction, slip a marker onto your right-hand needle. Insert your right-hand needle into the first stitch on the left-hand needle and work it.

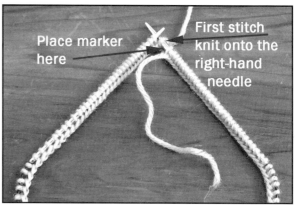

Place marker here

First stitch knit onto the right-hand needle

Photo 4: The marker is in place and the first stitch from the left-hand needle has been worked and now resides on the right-hand needle.

Which is the right and which is the left? Good question! The needle-tip with the "working yarn" (the yarn attached to the ball you will be working with), is the "right-hand needle" end. The needle-tip with the first Cast On stitch becomes the left-hand needle.

Compare the two examples of Cast On stitches in Photos 3 and 5 — they look slightly different because of the two methods of Cast On used.

Photo 3 has used the Long-Tail Cast On method and Photo 5 has used a two-needle knitting Cast On method.

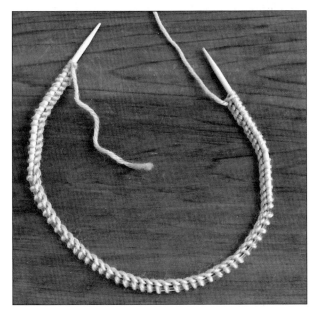

Photo 5: A knitted Cast On has the working yarn on the end of the right-hand needle and the end-tail on the left-hand needle.

Continue working the stitches around the needle (unless the pattern says otherwise you'll probably be using the knit stitch) until you reach the marker you placed earlier.

This is your last chance to check that your stitches are all straight on your needle. If you have noticed that your stitches are twisted around, adjust them now.

The Second Round: Slip the marker from the left-hand needle onto the right-hand needle without doing anything to the marker — it's simply there to let you know where one round ends and the next begins. Work the stitches around the needle to the marker.

If you are working Stocking Stitch then you would simply continue with the knit stitch, knitting every round — no purling.

It is not in the least unusual for the first stitch of the Cast On round to be looser than the other stitches on the round. Don't worry about this as it will neaten up very nicely when you sew

in the yarn end later. (But don't sew in this yarn end until later, as it can be useful to find the round beginning/end point if your marker falls off your needles at an early point in your work.)

ADVANTAGES OF KNITTING IN THE ROUND:

- Always facing the "right" side while you work
- Great for working repeating Fair Isle colour patterns
- Work sleeves down to the wrist - you can try the sweater on the wearer for a perfect sleeve length
- You can adjust the length of sleeves and body as you work
- For most knitters, faster to work
- And did we mention, NO SEWING?

KNITTING IN ONE PIECE

The cardigans in this book are knit with a circular needle, working back and forth, knitting on the right side and purling on the wrong side. This is a large piece of flat knitting worked in the same fashion as working smaller pieces on straight needles. A circular needle is used mainly because the number of stitches may become cumbersome on a straight needle.

After completing the collar you will be working the buttonband, front, sleeve, back, sleeve, front, and buttonband, ALL on one needle and at the same time. This method is quick and efficient. So no side seams or sleeve seams to sew, although there is an option for sewing the sleeve seam if you wish.

All the lengths can be adjusted as you work, because the garment is all together. You can try it on and adjust the length for your particular little one.

As you are working back and forth, knitting and purling, you can work any sort of intarsia colour pattern, or texture pattern, just as if the pieces were worked separately. This makes for interesting striping, picture knits and colour block options.

TECHNIQUES

For cardigans you will be working flat, or back and forth on a circular needle. When working flat, we refer to "rows" instead of "rounds".

The First Row: You will begin your first row by working the last stitch you Cast On. DO NOT join the stitches in a circle. Continue to work the stitches across the circular needle.

The Second Row: When you have reached the end of the row, simply turn your knitting over and continue working your piece beginning with the last stitch you worked. If you are working Stocking Stitch at this point you would purl the entire row to the end of the needle. If you are working Garter Stitch you would work this row again using the knit stitch.

When you are knitting flat pieces you can use straight needles, double-pointed needles or a circular needle. We like to use a circular needle; they're on hand because we use them a lot and as you knit the garment it sits in your lap rather than weighing down your elbows as you hold the garment-to-be up to work.

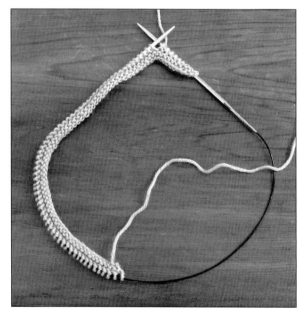

Photo 6: *A few rows of flat knitting on circular needles.*

When you finish the end of the row, you flip the needles over and begin again.

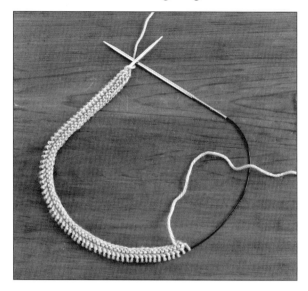

Photo 7: *Needles in position to begin the next row.*

ADVANTAGES OF KNITTING IN ONE PIECE - CARDIGAN

- You can work intarsia patterns

- No sewing of side seams — work the 2 fronts and the back together in one piece

- Work the sleeves down to the wrist — you can try it on for a perfect sleeve length, and adjust the length of the body as you progress

- Buttonhole bands are worked as you knit and not put on afterwards

- Collar is already attached.

- And did we mention, NO SEWING?

An Overview

THE LANGUAGE OF KNITTING

IT'S A BIG WORLD OUT THERE

There are certain differences in word usage in Canada, the United States, Europe, Australia, New Zealand and every other knitting-mad country.

Some examples include spelling (colour versus color), which are pretty easy to work out and other differences in actual words (in Canada we use Cast Off, but Bind Off is more usual in the U.S.) and there are wildly different needle sizes used.

So, to help out, the section Terms Used covers terminology used in the patterns and an explanation of differences.

MEASUREMENTS

We have included measurements in both imperial (inches) and metric (centimeters) in our patterns, along with yards and meters for yarn requirements.

Yarn weights are generally indicated in grams (i.e. 50g) but for clarification, a 100 gram ball is approximately 3 1/2 oz. One ounce equals 28.35 grams.

Additionally, needle sizes are indicated in both metric (ie 4.0mm) and US sizes (US6).

We think that covers it!

NEEDLE SIZES

For the most part, all of our patterns in this book are for DK (double knitting) weight yarn. This yarn knits to a gauge of 22 stitches for every 4"/10 cm on 4.0mm/US6 needles.

TERMS USED & ABBREVIATIONS

You say "tomato" and I say "tomato" ... as the song goes. Or, you say Bind Off and I say Cast Off. There are a number of differences in word usage among the various English speaking countries.

- **(curved brackets)** are used to indicate different instructions for different sizes. The smallest size is in front of the bracket and the larger sizes are inside the brackets. ie. 80 (88, 94) sts. Curved brackets are also used show that the instructions inside the brackets should be worked as a unit.

- **[square brackets]** indicates that whatever is inside the brackets should be worked the number of times indicated. So, if the instructions read: P1 [K4, P4] twice, you should: P1, K4, P4, K4, P4, ...

- **3-Needle Cast Off:** A method for casting off two edges of work at one time. See page 102 for instructions.

- **As established** or **as set** means to continue to work the stitch, cable or colour pattern as you have previously been instructed. Simply carry on with the pattern.

- **Backward Loop Increase:** Make an increase by putting a backward loop on the needle. See page 16 for instructions.

- **Ball band:** The paper label or tab that the yarn manufacturer puts on each ball of yarn. It is also referred to as a yarn wrapper.

   The ball band usually provides a range of information useful to the knitter, including the recommended gauge (sometimes referred to as tension) that the yarn knits to in stocking stitch, and the number of yards or metres in the ball.

- **Cast Off** is also known as bind-off and is the process of finishing the edge of a hem or sleeve cuff.

- **dpn(s)**: Double-point needle(s).

- **Dye lot**: Yarn is dyed in batches. All the balls of yarn of a colour with the same dye lot number were dyed in the same batch. When you are knitting a sweater or other garment all in one colour, please ensure that you have sufficient yarn with the same dye lot number to ensure even colour throughout the garment.

- **End with a wrong side row** means to continue with further instructions after you have completed working the wrong side row.

- **Fair Isle** is a repeating pattern with two or more colours, where all the colours of yarn are "carried" along the row or round where the pattern is used. Fair Isle work can be knit in the round (in fact it's much easier to knit a Fair Isle pattern in the round as you're always looking at the right-side of your work) or flat.

- **Garter Stitch:** When *Knitting Flat* you knit every row. When *Knitting in the Round* it is a two round sequence: knit one round and purl the next round.

- **Gauge or Tension**: The number of stitches over 1 or 4 inches (2.5 cm or 10 cm) of knitting obtained with a specific needle size, generally measured over stocking stitch unless otherwise indicated.

    A gauge over 4"/10 cm.
    22 sts = 4"/10 cm on US6 / 4.0mm needles
    A gauge over 1"/2.5 cm.
    5.5 sts = 1"/2.5 cm on US6 / 4.0mm needles

    10cm x 10cm

    30 ROWS

    22 STITCHES

The illustration is similar to what you'd see on a label or ball band, and represents a 4"/10 cm square. It shows the number of rows down the side of the graphic and the number of stitches along the bottom. Occasionally you will see a very similar graph without any indication of rows and stitches. If this is the case, you can assume that the smaller of the two numbers is the number of stitches per 4"/10 cm usually along the bottom of the graph, and the larger number is the number of rows per 4"/10 cm (in stocking stitch there are approximately 1.4 times more rows than stitches). It is important to know the recommended tension when you wish to substitute yarns. Not all yarns with the same ball band tension will be totally interchangeable as different fibre content can affect how the yarn works up, but it is a good starting point.

- **Inc:** Increase one stitch

- **Intarsia** is also a colour pattern but the colours are dropped at the edge of colour work and the colour is picked up and used again on the next row. This is often called picture knitting.

- **K2tog:** Knit two stitches together (right slanting decrease).

- **kw:** knitwise.

- **Left Front/Right Front:** means the left or right side of the front of the sweater as if you were wearing the garment.

- **P2tog:** Purl two stitches together.

- **Pick up and knit:** using the right needle, insert the needle through an edge stitch for example, and loop the wool around your needle as if you were knitting a stitch on the needle as usual. Complete the stitch by bringing the loop through to the right side. This makes a loop (stitch) on the right needle. This is often used so you can continue the knitting in a different direction without working separate pieces and sewing them together.

- **Place marker** and **Slip marker**: Placing a marker means to put the marker onto the right-hand needle. On the next round or row, you will work to a marker and "slip it" or move it from the left-hand needle onto the right-hand needle without doing anything to the marker. The short form for "place the marker" is **pm** and to "slip the marker" is **sm**.

- **pw:** purlwise.

- **Right Side (RS)** is the Public Side or the side that is facing out and will be seen when it is worn. **Wrong Side (WS)** is the side not shown to the public, and is next to your body.

- **SL1:** Slip one stitch. Slip the stitch from the left needle to the right needle without working the stitch. Unless instructed otherwise, the stitch is slipped as if to purl (insert your right-hand needle tip as if you are about to purl the stitch and slip it off the left-hand needle).

- **SSK:** Slip, slip, knit (left leaning decrease). Slip one stitch as if to knit, slip next stitch as if to knit, insert the left needle into the front of the two slipped stitches, from left to right, and knit them together.

- **Stocking stitch** is also known as stockinette stitch. When *Knitting Flat* it is a two row sequence: knit one row and purl one row. *When Knitting in the Round* you knit every round.

- **Stitch markers** are also known as "markers". A marker is a device (a piece of yarn tied in a circle, a coloured plastic or rubber ring, etc.) which you put on your needle to indicate a certain point in your knitting, such as the beginning of a round or the beginning or end of a panel of textured stitches, cable or colour pattern.

- **Yarn over** is a method for making an increase and creating a deliberate, decorative hole in the knitting. Yarn over can also be known as "overs". The short forms can appear as **yo** or **o**.

- **yo:** Bring wool under the right needle and forward to the front of your work, swing the wool over the right needle to the back of your work and knit the next stitch. The resulting loop is worked as if a stitch in the next row or round.

- **Yardage:** The length of yarn contained in a ball or skein. The pattern will indicate the number of balls used and the yardage of each ball. You will need to purchase the correct total amount of yards or meters to complete the garment. If a pattern calls for 50g of yarn, this is not an accurate representation of the quantity needed. Cotton, for example, is heavier than wool and 50g of cotton may not go as far as 50g of wool. The short form for yardage is **yds**.

INCREASES

There are a number of methods for increasing stitches. In most of the patterns you can choose any increase you like to use and in other instances the designer will give specific instructions in order to obtain a specific result. Check the pattern carefully.

Backward loop increase: Make an increase by putting a backward loop on the needle. It will be worked as a stitch in the next round.

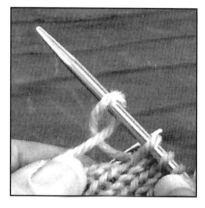

Photo 8: A backward loop prior to tightening it on the needle.

M1: Make one stitch (no holes). With the left needle lift the running thread between the stitch just worked and the next stitch, from front to back, and knit into the back of the resulting loop.

To be symmetrical, on the other side of the shapeline, with left needle lift the running thread from back to front, and knit the resulting loop. *(Note: This one is tighter to knit into.)*

Open M1: (with holes) Insert right needle under the running thread between the stitch just worked and next stitch without lifting or twisting it, wrap yarn around needle and bring to the front.

Kfb: Increase of 1 stitch also known as knitting into the front and back of a stitch. Knit into the front of the next stitch as usual and without taking the stitch off the left needle, knit into the back of the same stitch.

Yarn Over: Yarn over to make a hole (eyelet) and increase one stitch. Bring wool under the right needle and forward to the front of your work, swing the wool over the right needle to the back of your work, ready to work the next stitch.

Photo 9: The wool has been brought under the right needle and forward to the front of the work , then over the needle to the back in preparation to knit the next stitch.

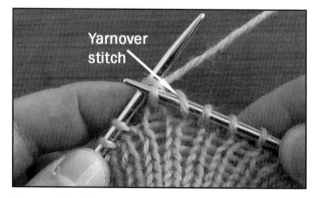

Photo 10: The next stitch being worked.

THE PATTERNS

THE BASIC PULLOVER

Experience Level: With Gusto!
(Enthusiastic Beginner)

designed by Deb Gemmell

ABBREVIATIONS:

Inc 1: Increase 1 stitch. See Increases on page 16 for descriptions of various increase methods.

pm: Place a marker.

sm: Slip the marker.

K2tog: Right slanting decrease. Knit the next two stitches together.

st(s): Stitch(es).

SSK: Left leaning decrease. Slip the next stitch as if to knit, slip the next stitch as if to knit, insert the left needle into the fronts of the two slipped stitches on the right needle. Knit the 2 slipped stitches together.

yo: Yarn over to make a hole (eyelet) and increase one stitch. Bring wool under the right needle and forward to the front of your work, swing the wool over the right needle to the back of your work, ready to work the next stitch. The resulting loop is knit in the next row.

This easy raglan pullover is knit in one piece from the top down with no sewing.

The yarn over increases used make counting the rounds easy but you have a choice of increasing with or without holes.

Needles:

5.0mm/US8 needle - Collar Cast On ONLY
4.0mm/US6 circular needle (40 cm/16" long)
Optional for two larger sizes:
4.0mm/US6 circular needle (60 cm/24" long)
1 set of 4.0mm/US6 double-point needles for the sleeves.

Tension:

22 stitches = 4"/10 cm on 4.0mm/US6 needle in stocking stitch or needle needed to obtain this tension.

To Fit:	1 year	2 year	4 year	6 year
Chest Size of:	20"	22"	24"	26"
	51 cm	56 cm	61 cm	66 cm
Finished Size:				
Chest	24"	26"	28"	30"
	61 cm	66 cm	71 cm	76 cm
Sleeve Length	6½"	8"	10"	12"
	16.5 cm	20.5 cm	25.5 cm	30.5 cm
Body Length	12"	13"	15"	17"
	30.5 cm	33 cm	38 cm	43 cm

Materials: DK Yarn 50g ball, 123m/135yds

	1 year	2 year	4 year	6 year
Main Colour	4	5	6	7
Ring markers	4	4	4	4

Directions are given for size 1, other sizes are in brackets. If only one figure is shown, it applies to all sizes.

The yarn used in the sample left is Magic Garden Buttons in colour #887.

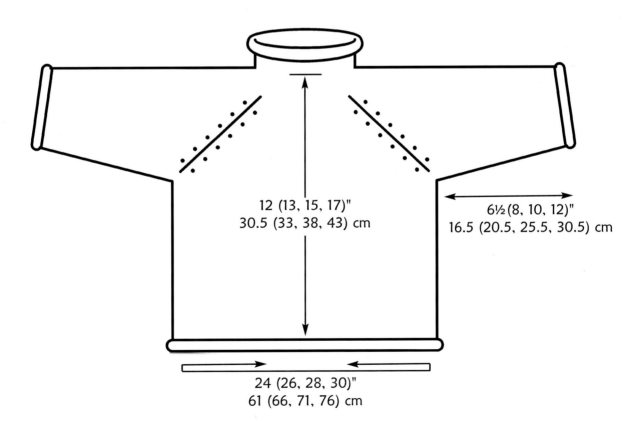

12 (13, 15, 17)"
30.5 (33, 38, 43) cm

6½ (8, 10, 12)"
16.5 (20.5, 25.5, 30.5) cm

24 (26, 28, 30)"
61 (66, 71, 76) cm

This basic pullover can be knit successfully using a variety of yarns, see below, for completely different effects.

We recommend you cast on with a larger needle to ensure the sweater will go over your small person's head easily. Then change to the body needle for the collar.

BEGIN AT THE COLLAR

With 5.0mm/US8 needle Cast On 72 (80, 88, 96) stitches.

Next Round: With smaller sized circular needle, knit the stitches off the larger needle.

Join in the round being careful not to twist your stitches. Place a marker to indicate the beginning of the round.

Knit every round for 1½ (1½, 2, 2)"/4 (4, 5, 5) cm.

YOKE

Four shapelines are used to increase on the yoke. Each shapeline consists of 2 stitches. Every other round, increases are worked before and after each of the shapelines. In the next round you will place a marker in the centre of the 4 shapelines.

Note: Make the First Marker different in some way (a different colour or tie a piece of coloured yarn to it) so that you will know where each round begins.

Marker Round: Slip First Marker, K1 (shapeline stitch), K26 (28, 30, 32) for the Body, K1 (shapeline stitch); Place Marker, K1 (shapeline stitch), K6 (8, 10, 12) for the sleeve, K1 (shapeline stitch); Place Marker, K1 (shapeline stitch), K26 (28, 30, 32) for the Body, K1 (shapeline stitch); Place Marker, K1 (shapeline stitch), K6 (8, 10, 12), K1 (shapeline stitch).

Yarns Used in order of appearance: Naturally Magic Garden Buttons, colour #887; Sirdar Snuggly Tiny Tots, colour #947; Butterfly Super 10 cotton, colour #3454; Sirdar Snuggly Domino, colour #763.

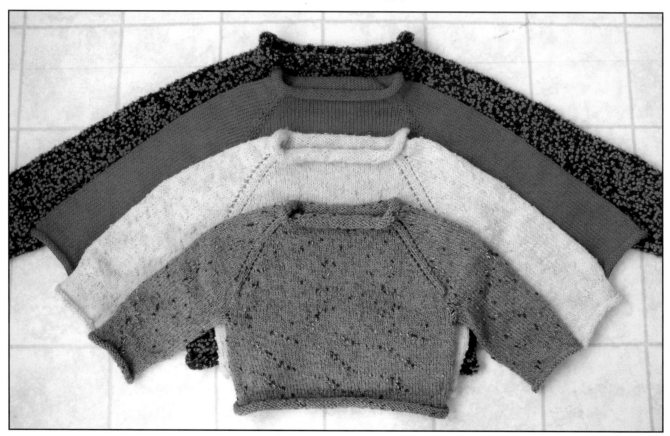

*Deb says: Increases are indicated by "Inc 1". Use the method of your choice or see the Increase section on page 16. I used the **yo** increase which is also described on page 16.*

Increase Round: *Slip marker, K1 (shapeline), Inc 1 stitch, knit to 1 stitch before next marker, Inc 1 stitch, K1; repeat from * around to First Marker.

Straight Round: Knit.

Repeat the last 2 rounds until you have 208 (232, 248, 264) stitches on your needle.

Note: Change to longer 4.0mm/US6 circular needle when the increased number of sts become too many for the shorter needle.

Reality Check: There should be 62 (68, 72, 76) stitches between the Markers for both the Body sections (includes the shapeline stitches). The sleeves should have 42 (48, 52, 56) stitches between the Markers. If you don't have this exact number don't worry about it, but try to fudge the numbers so that both the Body sections have the same number of stitches between the Markers, and both the sleeves have the same number.

If the Yoke is not yet 6 (7, 7½, 8)"/15 (18, 19, 20) cm deep, measuring vertically from the centre base of the collar down to your needle, continue to knit around without any more increases until you have reached the length above.

Divide Body and Sleeves: The Divide Round below will separate the sleeves and the body. The sleeve stitches will now be held on spare yarn as you work the Body first.

The Body stitches stay on the circular needle and stitches are cast on at the underarms.

At each shapeline, one shapeline stitch will go with the sleeve and one shapeline stitch with the Body stitches.

Divide Round: Remove markers as you go, *Knit to next marker (62, 68, 72, 76 Body stitches which stay on the circular needle); K42 (48, 52, 56) stitches to the next marker and thread the 42 (48, 52, 56) stitches just knit, onto a spare piece of yarn for the sleeve (sleeve stitches plus one shapeline stitch before

and after); repeat from * once more.   (124, 136, 144, 152 sts on needle for the Body.)

BODY

Next Round: Place a marker for the beginning of the round, knit to underarm, Cast On 4 (4, 5, 7) stitches, knit to underarm, Cast On 4 (4, 5, 7) stitches.   (132, 144, 154, 166 sts)

Knit every round until the sweater measures 10 (11, 13, 15)"/25.5 (28, 33, 38) cm from the base of collar down to needle or 2"/5 cm shy of desired length for the child you are making it for.

Next Round: Knit, decreasing 10 stitches evenly around the Body.

Knit every round for 2½"/6.5 cm. (The extra ½" is for the rolled edge.) **Cast Off**.

SLEEVES

Set-Up Round: With dp needles and RS facing, starting in the centre of the underarm stitches, pick up and knit 2 (2, 3, 4) stitches from the cast on edge of underarm stitches, pick up 1 extra stitch here at the corner to help close the gap, knit the sleeve stitches on spare yarn, pick up an extra stitch here at the corner to help close the gap, pick up and knit 2 (2, 2, 3) stitches to centre of underarm, place marker. (48, 54, 59, 65 sts)

Note: I don't think it is necessary to taper the sleeves for small children so I have put in directions for a straight sleeve for the 2 smallest sizes. However, with the instructions below you can taper the sleeves for all the sizes.

Straight sleeve (2 smaller sizes): Knit every round until sleeve measures 4½ (6)"/11.5 (15) cm or to 2"/5 cm shy of desired length for the recipient of the sweater.

Now work the Cuff.

- OR -

Taper the Sleeves (for all sizes):

Set-Up Round: (Sizes 1 & 2 ONLY) Inc 1 stitch, knit to end of round. (49, 55 stitches) The increased stitch becomes the underarm seamline stitch.

All sizes: Knit 7 rounds.

Next and every 8th round: K1, SSK, knit to 2 stitches before the end of the round, K2tog.

Repeat the last 8 rounds (Do not decrease to less than 41, 41, 45, 45 stitches), until sleeve measures 4½ (6, 8, 10)"/11.5 (15, 20.5, 25.5) cm from the underarm or to 2"/5 cm shy of desired length for the recipient of the sweater.

Now work the Cuff.

CUFF

Next Round (Straight Sleeve — 2 small sizes): K2tog, *K4 (2), K2tog; repeat 6 (12) times, ending with K4 (0). (40, 40 sts)

Next Round (Tapered Sleeve): Knit, decreasing to 40 (40, 44, 44) stitches.

Knit every round for 2½"/6.5 cm. (The extra ½"/1.5 cm is for the rolled edge.) **Cast Off.**

Sew in ends so that they can not be seen when the edges roll.

THE BASIC CARDIGAN

Experience Level: With Gusto!
(Enthusiastic Beginner)

designed by Dana Gibbons

ABBREVIATIONS:

Inc 1: Increase 1 stitch. See Increases at the end of the book for descriptions of various increase methods.

K2tog: Right slanting decrease. Knit the next two stitches together.

Kfb: Increase by knitting into the front and back of a stitch.

pm: Place a marker.

sm: Slip the marker.

SSK: Left leaning decrease. Slip the next stitch as if to knit, slip the next stitch as if to knit, insert the left needle into the fronts of the two slipped stitches on the right needle. Knit the 2 slipped stitches together.

yo: Yarn over to make a hole (eyelet) and increase one stitch. Bring wool under the right needle and forward to the front of your work, swing the wool over the right needle to the back of your work, ready to work the next stitch. The resulting loop is purled in the next row.

This easy raglan is knit in one piece from the top down with a minimum of finishing.

You can knit the sleeves in the round with double-pointed needles, or there is an option to knit them flat and sew up later.

The yarn over increases are attractive and also make counting the rows easy.

With buttonholes on both bands, it's ready for a boy or girl.

Needles:

4.0mm/US6 circular needle (24"/60 cm long)
4.0mm/US6 double-point needles (for "no sew" sleeves)

Tension:

22 stitches = 4"/10 cm on 4.0mm/US6 needle in stocking stitch or needle needed to obtain this tension.

To Fit:	1 year	2 year	4 year	6 year
Chest Size of:	20"	22"	24"	26"
	51 cm	56 cm	61 cm	66 cm
Finished Size:				
Chest	24"	26"	29"	31"
	61 cm	66 cm	73.5 cm	79 cm
Sleeve Length	6½"	8"	10"	12"
	16.5 cm	20.5 cm	25.5 cm	30.5 cm
Body Length	12"	13"	15"	17"
	30.5 cm	33 cm	38 cm	43 cm

Materials: DK yarn - 50g ball, 119m/130yds

Main Colour	4	5	6	7
Ring markers	6	6	6	6
Shank Buttons (15mm)	5	6	6	7
Shirt Buttons (2-hole)	5	6	6	7

Buttonhole twist thread

Directions are given for size 1, other sizes are in brackets. If only one figure is shown, it applies to all sizes.

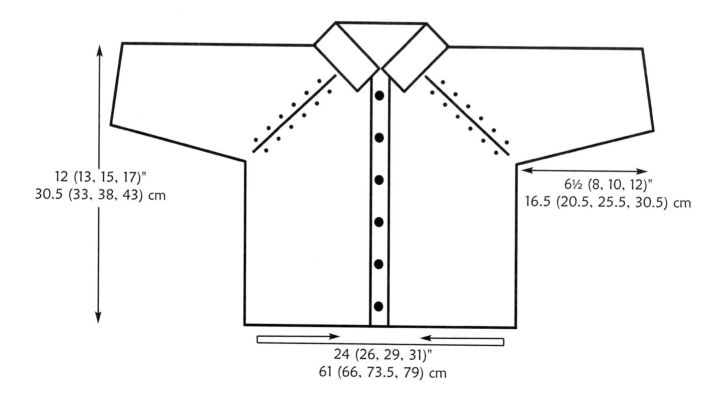

12 (13, 15, 17)"
30.5 (33, 38, 43) cm

6½ (8, 10, 12)"
16.5 (20.5, 25.5, 30.5) cm

24 (26, 29, 31)"
61 (66, 73.5, 79) cm

The Basic Cardigan

BEGIN AT THE COLLAR

With circular needle **Cast On** 64 (72, 78, 84) stitches.

Work back and forth on the circular needle, in Garter Stitch (knit every row), for 2½ (3, 3, 3¼)"/6 (7.5, 7.5, 8) cm, ending after a RS row.

COLLAR SHAPING:

Row 1: With WS facing, K4, [K2tog] 28 (32, 35, 38) times, K4. (36, 40, 43, 46 sts)

Row 2: (RS) K4, P28 (32, 35, 38), K4.

Row 3: Knit.

Row 4: K4, P28 (32, 35, 38), K4.

Row 5: K4, [knit into the front and back (Kfb) of next stitch] 28 (32, 35, 38) times, K4. (64, 72, 78, 84 sts)

Row 6: K4, P56 (64, 70, 76), K4.

Note: This collar is flipped over when worn so that the even numbered rows are showing when the sweater is on. The RS for the rest of the cardigan is indicated in the instructions.

YOKE

We are now going to set up 4 shapelines for the raglan shoulder shaping. Markers will be set between the two knit stitches of the shapelines. Eyelet yarn over increases will be worked before and after each of the shapelines. Stitches for the button bands are also added now.

Yarns Used in order of appearance: *Naturally Magic Garden Buttons colour #5848; Wendy Rembrant in Jade, #3504; Classic Elite Flash cotton in Lotus Blossom, #3454; the navy was from Deb and Lynda's stash.*

LET'S BEGIN

Row 1: (RS) Cast On 5 stitches (for left button band), knit these 5 stitches, place marker (pm), K10 (12, 13, 14) stitches for left Front, yo, K1, pm, K1, yo, K8 (8, 9, 10) stitches for sleeve, yo, K1, pm, K1, yo, K20 (24, 26, 28) stitches for Back, yo, K1, pm, K1, yo, K8 (8, 9, 10) stitches for sleeve, yo, K1, pm, K1, yo, K10 (12, 13, 14) stitches for right Front.

Row 2: Cast on 5 stitches (right button band), knit these 5 stitches, pm, purl to last marker, purling loops of yo increase, K5. (82, 90, 96, 102 sts)

Row 3: (RS) K5, slip marker (sm), *knit to 1 stitch before next marker, yo, K1, sm, K1, yo; repeat from * 3 more times, knit to end of row. (increase of 8 stitches - 90, 98, 104, 110 stitches)

Row 4: K5, purl to last 5 stitches, K5.

Repeat Rows 3 and 4 twice more (increasing at shapeline markers as set).

Buttonholes are now placed on both the right and left buttonbands. The buttons will be sewn over the holes on the appropriate buttonband, which ensures that the buttons and the button-holes will line up perfectly.

Buttonhole Row: (RS) K1, K2tog, yo, K2, sm, *knit to 1 stitch before next marker, yo, K1, sm, K1, yo; repeat from * 3 more times, knit to last 5 stitches, sm, K2, yo, K2tog, K1.

Next Row: (WS) K5, purl to last 5 stitches, K5.

Repeat Rows 3 and 4 above, increasing as set, making buttonholes after every 9 (10, 10, 10) Garter Stitch ridges (every 18, 20, 20, 20 rows). The buttonholes will sit between the ridges.

Continue until you can count 20 (22, 24, 26) pairs of eyelets along the raglan shapelines, ending after a WS row. (234, 258, 280, 302 sts)

Don't forget your buttonholes!

Work 2 rows even without increases, ending after a WS row.

SLEEVES

We now have 2 methods for completing the sleeves.

- Working the sleeves in the round on double-point needles, with "no sew" finishing;

  OR

- Working the sleeve stitches back and forth on the circular needle and sewing up the sleeve seam.

It's your choice!

SLEEVE METHOD 1: in the Round.

Divide Body and first Sleeve: (RS) Knit across 36 (40, 43, 46) stitches of left Front ; knit next 50 (54, 59, 64) stitches onto double-point needles for the sleeve, dividing these stitches evenly on the needles.

Join sleeve stitches in the round, place marker at beginning of the round.

Knit 5 (5, 7, 7) rounds.

Decrease Round: K1, K2tog, knit to last 3 stitches, SSK, K1.

Repeat last 6 (6, 8, 8) rounds until sleeve measures 5½ (7, 9, 11)"/14 (18, 23, 28) cm from dividing row.

Next Round: Purl, decreasing evenly to 38 (38, 39, 40) stitches, if necessary.

CUFF

Next Round: Knit.

Next Round: Purl.

Repeat last 2 rounds until there are 5 (5, 6, 6) Garter Stitch ridges, ending with a knit round.

With RS facing, **Cast Off** while purling.

Divide for second sleeve: Attach yarn and knit across 62 (70, 76, 82) stitches to next marker, knit 50 (54, 59, 64) stitches for next sleeve onto double-point needles, dividing equally among the double-point needles.

Work same as first sleeve.

Finish Dividing Row: Attach yarn and knit remaining stitches from right Front. (134, 150, 162, 174 stitches on circular needle for Body)

Continue with Body.

SLEEVE METHOD 2: worked Flat.

Divide Body and Sleeve: (RS) Knit across 36 (40, 43, 46) stitches of Front; knit next 50 (54, 59, 64) stitches of sleeve, Turn.

Next Row: P50 (54, 59, 64) stitches for sleeve.

Working back and forth on sleeve stitches, work 4 (4, 6, 6) rows in Stocking Stitch.

Decrease Row: (RS) K1, K2tog, knit to last 3 stitches, SSK, K1.

Work 5 (5, 7, 7) rows in Stocking Stitch.

Repeat last 6 (6, 8, 8) rows until sleeve measures 5½ (7, 9, 11)"/14 (18, 23, 28) cm from dividing row, ending after a RS row.

Next Row: (WS) Knit, decreasing evenly to 38 (38, 39, 40) stitches, if necessary.

CUFF

Knit every row until there are 5 (5, 6, 6) Garter Stitch ridges showing on the RS, end after knitting a RS row.

With WS facing, **Cast Off** knitwise. Cut yarn.

Divide for second Sleeve: Attach yarn and knit across 62 (70, 76, 82) stitches of Back to next marker; knit next 50 (54, 59, 64) stitches for sleeve, Turn.

Work as for first sleeve.

Finish Dividing Row: Attach yarn and knit remaining stitches of right Front to end of row. (134, 150, 162, 174 stitches on circular needle for Body)

BODY

Row 1: (WS) K5, purl to first sleeve junction, pick up 2 stitches to close gaps, purl to next sleeve junction, pick up 2 stitches, purl to last 5 stitches, K5.

Row 2: (RS) Knit to extra underarm stitches, K2tog, knit to extra underarm stitches, K2tog, knit to end of row. (136, 152, 164, 176 sts)

Row 3: K5, purl to last 5 stitches, K5.

Row 4: (RS) Knit.

Row 5: K5, purl to last 5 stitches, K5.

Repeat last 2 rows (4 and 5) continuing to work buttonholes every 9 (10, 10, 10) Garter Stitch ridges, until the sweater measures 11 (12, 14, 16)"/28 (30.5, 35.5, 40.5) cm measuring down the centre back from the base of the collar to your needle, ending after a WS row. You can lengthen the sweater here and work to 1"/2 cm shy of desired length.

GARTER STITCH BORDER

Knit every row until you have 5 (5, 6, 6) ridges showing on RS, end after knitting a RS row.

With WS facing, **Cast Off** knitwise.

FINISHING

Sew sleeve seams if necessary, closing gap at underarm.

Weave in ends.

Sew buttons over the buttonholes on the Left Band for girls or Right Band for boys.

Block if necessary.

THE BASIC HAT

designed by Lynda Gemmell

Experience Level: With Gusto!
(Enthusiastic Beginner)

Needles: 4.0mm/US6 circular needle (16"/40)
4.0mm/US6 double-point needles

STARTING AT THE TOP WITH I-CORD

With a 4.0mm/US6 dp needle Cast On 4 sts.

Using 2 double-pointed needles, I-cord for
1"/2.5 cm OR I-cord for 5"/12.5 cm and tie in a
knot when finished. (See page 102 for I-Cord
instructions)

After the last round, redistribute the stitches
onto two double-point needles and use a third
needle to knit with. Mark the beginning of
your round by putting a safety pin through the
first stitch of the round.

Now work in the round.

*Note: Redistribute the stitches onto more dp
needles as you increase and to a 16"/40 cm circular
needle when you can.*

Increase Round: Work [K1, Inc 1] to end of
round. (8 sts)

Knit 2 rounds.

Increase Round: Work [K1, Inc 1] to end of
round. (16 sts)

Knit 2 rounds.

To Fit:

	1 year	2 year	4 year	6 year
Finished Size	17½"	17½"	18"	19"
	44.5 cm	44.5 cm	46 cm	48 cm

Materials: DK yarn - 50g ball, 119m/130yds

Main Colour	1	1	1	1

Increase Round: Work [K1, Inc 1] to end of
round. (32 sts)

Knit 3 rounds.

Increase Round: Work [K2, Inc 1] to end of
round. (48 sts)

Knit 4 rounds.

Increase Round: Work [K3, Inc 1] to end of
round. (64 sts)

Knit 4 rounds.

Increase Round: Work [K4, Inc 1] to end of
round. (80 sts)

Knit 4 rounds.

Increase Round: Work [K5, Inc 1] to end of
round. (96 sts)

Knit 4 rounds.

BODY OF HAT

Increase Round: Knit, increasing 0 (0, 4, 8)
stitches evenly across round. (96, 96, 100, 104 sts)

Knit every round for 4 (4¼, 4½, 5)"/10 (11,
11.5, 12.5) cm. The last inch of the hat will roll
up and form the brim.

*Note: If you would like the rolled brim to be
tighter, change to a circular needle one size smaller
to work the last 2"/5 cm of the Body above.*

Using the larger needle, Cast Off all stitches.

Sew in the ends. The end of the cast off round
should be sewn in on the RS, so that when the
brim is rolled up it won't show.

*The Basic Hat was knit in Emu Superwash
wool #1112.*

JAZZ IT UP!

Consider the possibilities! You can do so much with the two basic sweater patterns.

You can also reverse the arrangements you see above. The Basic Cardigan looks terrific when the entire cardigan is knit in eyelash - think of the look of a faux fur coat! And, The Basic Pullover would look very nice with eyelash trim at the neck, cuff and hem.

Let your imagination go wild!

The inspiration for the snazzy, jazzy wool and eyelash cardigan (left above) came from Karen Lawrence. Karen owns SheepStrings, a terrific yarn shop in Huntsville, Ontario.

*Note: Eyelash yarn comes in many weights. **Please ensure you are using the correct weight of eyelash.** Look on the ball band/yarn wrapper for the tension, which should read 22 sts = 4"/10 cm on a US6/4.0mm needle - OR - 5½ sts = 1"/2.5 cm on a US6/4.0mm needle.*

The above garments were knit using Stylecraft Eskimo DK eyelash in purple #5244 and Emu Superwash wool in purple #3633.

THE BASIC CARDIGAN WITH EYELASH TRIM

THE CARDIGAN WITH EYELASH TRIM

2 - 50g balls of DK weight eyelash for trim.

BEGIN AT THE COLLAR

With DK eyelash yarn, **Cast on** the number of stitches as indicated in The Basic Cardigan pattern.

Work back and forth on the circular needle, in Garter Stitch (knit every row), for 3 (3½, 3½, 4)"/7.5 (9, 9, 10) cm, ending after a RS row.

Note: We like to make the collar of the cardigan a little deeper when using eyelash as the yarn tends to "bulk up" a bit and needs the extra length.

Continue following The Basic Cardigan pattern for the collar.

YOKE

At this point cut the eyelash yarn and CHANGE to your regular knitting yarn of choice and follow pattern until you reach the cuff of the first SLEEVE.

SLEEVE METHOD 1: in the Round.

Cuff in eyelash:

You have decreased to 38 (38, 39, 40) sts on needle. Break yarn and **change** to eyelash yarn.

Next round: With eyelash yarn, knit.

Next Round: Purl.

Repeat last 2 rounds until there are 5 (5, 6, 6) Garter Stitch ridges, ending with a knit round.

With RS facing, **Cast Off** while purling. Cut yarn.

SLEEVE METHOD 2: worked Flat.

Cuff in eyelash:

Cut yarn and **change** to eyelash yarn.

With eyelash yarn, knit every row until there are 5 (5, 6, 6) Garter Stitch ridges showing on the RS, end after knitting a RS row.

With WS facing, **Cast Off** knitwise. Cut yarn.

Continue with The Basic Cardigan pattern until you reach the bottom of the BODY and the sweater measures 11 (12, 14, 16)"/28 (30.5, 35.5, 40.5) cm measuring down the centre back from the base of the collar to your needle, ending after a WS row. You can lengthen the sweater here and work to 1"/2.5 cm shy of desired length.

Break the body yarn and **change** to eyelash yarn.

With eyelash yarn, knit every row until you have 5 (5, 6, 6) ridges showing on RS, end after knitting a RS row.

With WS facing, **Cast Off** knitwise.

BASICS ENTIRELY IN EYELASH

THE EYELASH PULLOVER

Follow The Basic Pullover pattern as set using DK eyelash yarn.

THE EYELASH CARDIGAN

Follow The Basic Cardigan pattern, as set, using an eyelash yarn with the one change as noted below:

COLLAR

With eyelash yarn, **Cast on** the number of stitches as indicated in pattern.

Work back and forth on the circular needle, in Garter Stitch (knit every row), for 3 (3½, 3½, 4)"/7.5 (9, 9, 10) cm, ending after a RS row.

Note: We like to make the collar of the cardigan a little deeper when using eyelash as the yarn tends to "bulk up" a bit and needs the extra length.

Now Continue following The Basic Cardigan pattern to the end.

THE BASIC SOCK

This pattern is written for a set of 5dp needles. You will need to adjust the number of stitches on each needle if you are using a 4 needle set.

With such little socks, the "shortie", 5"/12.5 cm needle sets are ideal.

BEGIN WITH THE CUFF

Cast On 36 (36, 40, 40) stitches loosely. (It's important to cast on loosely so the very top row of the sock has lots of give.) Divide stitches evenly onto four needles. Join in the round, being careful not to twist the stitches.

TOP OF SOCK

Work [K2, P2] for 3½ (4, 4, 4½)"/9 (10, 10, 11.5) cm.

Knit 2 rounds.

HEEL FLAP

This is the "back" or flap of the sock heel.

Knit 9 (9, 10, 10) sts across the 1st needle, Turn.

Work onto a single needle: Sl1, P17 (17, 19, 19) stitches.

Reality Check: *You now have one needle with 18 (18, 20, 20) stitches for the heel flap and two needles of 9 (9, 10, 10) each for the instep.*

The two needles with 9 (9, 10, 10) stitches each are held for the instep. You won't use these stitches until you complete the back of the heel.

Work back and forth on the 18 (18, 20, 20) stitches for the heel, starting with the RS facing:

1st Row: (RS) Work [Sl1, K1] to end of row, Turn.

2nd Row: Sl1, then purl to the end of the row, Turn.

Repeat these two rows until work measures 1¾ (1¾, 2, 2)"/4.5 (4.5, 5, 5) cm from end of ribbing, ending after a WS row.

TURNING THE HEEL

Row 1: (RS) Knit 9 (9, 10, 10) to the centre of the heel, then knit 4 sts beyond, SSK, Turn.

Row 2: Sl1, P8, P2tog, Turn.

To Fit:	1 year	2 year	4 year	6 year
Foot Finished Size	4½" 11.5 cm	5½" 14 cm	6½" 16.5 cm	7½" 19 cm

Materials: DK yarn - 50g ball, 119m/130yds; DK Eyelash - 50g ball, 90m/98yds

	1 year	2 year	4 year	6 year
Main Colour	1	1	1	1
Eyelash	1	1	1	1

designed by Lynda Gemmell

Experience Level: With Gusto!
(Enthusiastic Beginner)

Needles:
1 set of 3.25mm/US3 double-point needles

Tension:
24 stitches = 4"/10 cm on 3.25mm/US3 needle in stocking stitch or needle needed to obtain this tension.
The YARN BALL BAND/yarn wrapper should read: 22 sts = 4"/10 cm on 4 mm/US6 needles.

Row 3: Sl1, K8, SSK, Turn.

Row 4: Sl1, P8, P2tog, Turn.

Repeat last 2 rows until all side stitches have been worked, ending after completing a WS row. (You should have 10 sts left on this needle.)

Knit 5 stitches to the middle of the heel.

THE HEEL GUSSET

Now that you're picking up stitches along the heel flap you are back to using 4 needles and knitting with the 5th.

Set-Up Round: Using a new needle, knit next 5 stitches and with the same needle, pick up and K9 (10, 11, 11) stitches along the right side of heel; work across instep stitches (keeping them on the two needles); then with the fifth needle, pick up and K9 (10, 11, 11) stitches along left side of heel and work across the remaining 5 heel stitches. You should have 14 (15, 16, 16) stitches on the first needle, the second and third needles should each have 9 (9, 10, 10) instep stitches, and the fourth should have 14 (15, 16, 16) stitches. If not, adjust your stitches to achieve this.

The round now begins at the centre back of the heel.

SHAPE THE GUSSET

Round 1: Work to last 3 stitches on the 1st needle, K2tog, K1; work across both the 2nd and 3rd needles (instep stitches); at the beginning of the 4th needle, K1, SSK, work to end.

Round 2: Knit.

Repeat these 2 rounds, decreasing at the end of the 1st needle and the beginning of the 4th needle, until you have a total of 36 (36, 40, 40) sts.

Knit every round on these stitches until the foot measures approximately 2 (3, 4, 5)"/5 (7.5, 10, 12.5) cm from beginning of heel gusset.

SHAPE THE TOE

Round 1: Knit to last 3 stitches on the first needle, K2tog, K1; at the beginning of the second needle K1, SSK, knit to end of needle; knit to last 3 stitches on the third needle and K2tog, K1; on the fourth needle K1, SSK, knit to end of needle - 32 (32, 36, 36) stitches.

Round 2: Knit.

The Basic Socks were knit in Regia 6 Crazy Color #5260.

Work these 2 rounds until 20 stitches remain.

Repeat Round 1 only, until there are 8 stitches remaining.

Thread the end of the yarn onto a blunt-pointed sewing needle and pass the yarn through all the remaining stitches; pull them tight and secure.

Sew in the ends and you're done!

The Basic Sock

THE RUSSIAN HAT

STARTING AT THE TOP WITH I-CORD

With MC and 2 dp needles, **Cast On** 4 stitches and work I-cord for 4 rows. See page 102 for I-Cord instructions.

WHEEL OF HAT

The wheel has 8 sections. You will be increasing 8 sts every second round. Change to a circular needle when you can unless you prefer dp needles.

Increase for wheel of hat:

Use an increase of your choice.

Increase Round: With MC, work [K1, Inc 1] to end of round. (8 sts on needles)

Distribute stitches onto your set of double-point needles and work in the round.

Note: You may find it easier to distribute onto 2 double-point needles and knit with a third needle at this point and then distribute onto your full set of double-point needles after you have 16 or 24 sts.

Next Round: Knit 1 round.

Increase Round: Work [K1, Inc 1] to end of round. (16 sts)

Next Round: Knit 1 round.

Increase Round: Work [K2, Inc 1] to end of round. (24 sts)

Next Round: Knit 1 round.

Increase Round: Work [K3, Inc 1] to end of round. (32 sts)

Next round: Knit 1 round.

Increase Round: Work [K4, Inc 1] to end of round.

Next Round: Knit 1 round.

Continue increasing at the end of each of the 8 sections every 2nd round, until you have a total of 96 (96, 96, 104) stitches. Break yarn. (12, 12, 12, 13 sts in each of the 8 sections).

BODY OF HAT

Change to DK eyelash yarn.

Knit 1 round increasing 0 (0, 4, 0) stitches evenly across round. (96, 96, 100, 104 sts)

To Fit:

To Fit:	1 year	2 year	4 year	6 year
Finished Size	17½"	17½"	18"	19"
	44.5 cm	44.5 cm	46 cm	48 cm

Materials: DK yarn - 50g ball, 119m/130yds; DK Eyelash - 50g ball, 90m/98yds

Main Colour	1	1	1	1
Eyelash	1	1	1	1

designed by Dana Gibbons

Experience Level: With Gusto!
(Enthusiastic Beginner)

Needles:
4.0mm/US6 circular needle (16"/40)
4.0mm/US6 double-point needles

Purl 1 round for ridge.

Knit 1 round.

Knit every round until it measures 2½ (3, 3½, 4)"/6.5 (7.5, 9, 10) cm.

BOTTOM EDGE

Using DK eyelash yarn, work [K2, P2] for ½"/1.5 cm.

Cast off in rib. You may want to use a 4.5mm/US7 needle to cast off for a looser edge. Sew in ends.

FLOWER

With MC, Cast on 60 stitches.

Knit 1 row.

Cast off knitwise.

Cut yarn leaving a long tail (approx 8"/20 cm). Sew ends of the flower together making a circle. Take yarn and run through the 12th stitch from beginning and draw tight. This pulls the stitches into a loop (first petal). Repeat this (every 12th stitch) 4 more times, creating 5 petals.

Sew a few more stitches in the center to fix the flower. Affix the button (optional) into the center then sew on to hat.

Create a tassel (see page 53) and sew on to hat.

LITTLE VIKING

Experience Level: Intermediate

adapted By Megan Lacey

ABBREVIATIONS:

Inc 1: Increase 1 stitch. See Increases on page 16 for descriptions of various increase methods.

K2tog: Right slanting decrease. Knit the next two stitches together.

Kfb: Increase by knitting into the front and back of a stitch.

pm: Place a marker.

sm: Slip the marker.

st(s): Stitch(es).

SSK: Left leaning decrease. Slip the next stitch as if to knit, slip the next stitch as if to knit, insert the left needle into the fronts of the two slipped stitches on the right needle. Knit the 2 slipped stitches together.

yo: Yarn Over to make a hole (eyelet) and increase one stitch.

Megan has given the traditional Nordic style a new and colourful twist for little Vikings everywhere. We love it in poster-paint brights, or go for that junior preppy look in pale pastels.

Needles:

4.0mm/US6 circular needle (24"/60 cm long)
4.0mm/US6 double-point needles (for "no sew" sleeves)

Tension:

22 stitches = 4"/10 cm on 4.0mm/US6 needle in stocking stitch or needle needed to obtain this tension.

Directions are given for size 1, other sizes are in brackets. If only one figure is shown, it applies to all sizes.

To Fit:	1 year	2 year	4 year	6 year
Chest Size of:	20"	22"	24"	26"
	51 cm	56 cm	61 cm	66 cm
Finished Size:				
Chest	24"	26"	29"	31"
	61 cm	66 cm	74 cm	79 cm
Sleeve Length	6½"	8"	10"	12"
	16.5 cm	20.5 cm	25.5 cm	30.5 cm
Body Length	12"	13"	15"	17"
	30.5 cm	33 cm	38 cm	43 cm

Materials: DK Yarn - 50g ball, 119m/130yds

	1 year	2 year	4 year	6 year
Main Colour	4	4	5	5
Contrast Colour 1	½	½	½	½
Contrast Colour 2	½	½	½	½
Contrast Colour 3	¼	¼	¼	¼
Ring markers	6	6	6	6
Shank Buttons (15mm)	5	6	6	7
Shirt Buttons (2-hole)	5	6	6	7

Buttonhole twist thread

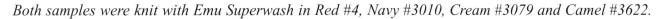

Both samples were knit with Emu Superwash in Red #4, Navy #3010, Cream #3079 and Camel #3622.

BEGIN AT THE COLLAR

With Main Colour **Cast On** 64 (72, 78, 84) sts.

Work back and forth on the circular needle, in Garter Stitch (knit every row) in Stripe Pattern as follows:

With Main Colour, knit 4 rows (makes 2 Garter Stitch ridges).

Note: Knit the next 6 rows, in stripes as follows, your choice of Contrast and Main Colours. The collars on the previous pages show two different choices.

Red sweater sample:

> With CC2, Knit 2 rows (1 ridge).
> With MC, Knit 2 rows (1 ridge).
> With CC1, Knit 2 rows (1 ridge).

Next Row: (RS) With MC, Knit.

Continue to knit every row, in MC, until collar measures 2½ (3, 3, 3¼)"/6.5 (7.5, 7.5, 8) cm, ending after a RS row.

COLLAR SHAPING

Row 1: With WS facing, K4, [K2tog] 28 (32, 35, 38) times, K4. (36, 40, 43, 46 sts)

Row 2: (RS) K4, P28 (32, 35, 38), K4.

Row 3: Knit.

Row 4: K4, P28 (32, 35, 38), K4.

Row 5: K4, [knit into the front and back (Kfb) of next stitch] 28 (32, 35, 38) times, K4. (64, 72, 78, 84 sts)

Row 6: K4, P56 (64, 70, 76), K4.

Note: This collar is flipped over when worn so that the even numbered rows are showing when the sweater is on. The RS for the rest of the coat is indicated in the instructions.

YOKE

We are now going to set up 4 shapelines for the raglan shoulder shaping. Markers will be set between the 2 knit stitches of the shapelines. Eyelet yarn over increases will be worked before and after each of the shapelines. Stitches for the button bands are also added now.

LET'S BEGIN

Row 1: (RS) Cast On 5 stitches (for left button band), knit these 5 stitches, place marker (pm), K10 (12, 13, 14) stitches for left Front, yo, K1, pm, K1, yo, K8 (8, 9, 10) stitches for sleeve, yo, K1, pm, K1, yo, K20 (24, 26, 28) stitches for Back, yo, K1, pm, K1, yo, K8 (8, 9, 10) stitches for sleeve, yo, K1, pm, K1, yo, K10 (12, 13, 14) stitches for right Front.

Row 2: Cast on 5 stitches (right button band), knit the 5 stitches, pm, purl to last marker, purling loops of yo increase, K5. (82, 90, 96, 102 sts)

Row 3: (RS) K5, slip marker (sm), *knit to 1 stitch before next marker, yo, K1, sm, K1, yo; repeat from * 3 more times, knit to end of row. (increase of 8 stitches-90, 98, 104, 110 stitches)

Row 4: K5, purl to last 5 stitches, K5.

Repeat Rows 3 and 4 twice more (increasing at shapeline markers as set).

Buttonholes are now placed on both the right and left buttonbands. The buttons will be sewn over the holes on the appropriate buttonband, which ensures that the buttons and the buttonholes will line up perfectly.

Buttonhole Row: (RS) K1, K2tog, yo, K2, sm, *knit to 1 stitch before next marker, yo, K1, sm, K1, yo; repeat from * 3 more times, knit to last 5 stitches, sm, K2, yo, K2tog, K1.

Next Row: (WS) K5, purl to last 5 stitches, K5.

Repeat Rows 3 and 4 above, increasing as set, making buttonholes after every 9 (10, 10, 10) garter stitch ridges (every 18, 20, 20, 20 rows). The buttonholes will sit between the ridges.

Continue until you can count 20 (22, 24, 26) pairs of eyelets along the raglan shapelines, ending after a WS row. (234, 258, 280, 302 sts)

Don't forget your buttonholes!

Work 2 rows without increases, ending after a WS row.

SLEEVES

We now have 2 options for completing the sleeves.

1) Working the sleeves in the round on double-point needles, with "no sew" finishing.

2) Working the sleeve stitches back and forth on the circular needle and sewing up the sleeve seam.

It's your choice!

SLEEVE METHOD 1: IN THE ROUND.

Divide Body and first Sleeve: (RS) Knit across 36 (40, 43, 46) stitches of left Front; knit next 50 (54, 59, 64) stitches onto double-point needles for the sleeve, dividing these stitches evenly on the needles.

Join sleeve stitches in the round, place marker at beginning of the round.

Knit 5 (5, 7, 7) rounds.

Decrease Round: K1, K2tog, knit to last 3 stitches, SSK, K1.

Repeat last 6 (6, 8, 8) rounds until sleeve measures 5½ (7, 9, 11)"/14 (18, 23, 28) cm from dividing row.

Next Round: Purl, decreasing evenly to 38 (38, 39, 40) stitches, if necessary.

Next Round: Knit.

Next Round: Purl.

Repeat last 2 rounds until there are 5 (5, 6, 6) Garter Stitch ridges, ending with a knit round.

With RS facing, Cast Off while purling.

Divide for second sleeve: Attach yarn and knit across 62 (70, 76, 82) stitches to next marker, knit 50 (54, 59, 64) stitches for next sleeve onto double-point needles, dividing equally among the double-point needles.

Work same as first sleeve.

Finish Dividing Row: Attach yarn and knit remaining stitches from right Front. (134, 150, 162, 174 sts on circular needle for Body)

SLEEVE METHOD 2: WORKED FLAT.

Divide Body and Sleeve: (RS) Knit across 36 (40, 43, 46) stitches of Front; knit next 50 (54, 59, 64) stitches of sleeve, Turn.

Row 2: P50 (54, 59, 64) stitches for sleeve.

Working back and forth on sleeve stitches, work 4 (4, 6, 6) rows in Stocking Stitch.

Decrease Row: (RS) K1, K2tog, knit to last 3 stitches, SSK, K1.

Work 5 (5, 7, 7) rows in Stocking Stitch.

Repeat last 6 (6, 8, 8) rows until sleeve measures 5½ (7, 9, 11)"/14 (18, 23, 28) cm from dividing row, ending after a RS row.

Next Row: (WS) Knit, decreasing evenly to 38 (38, 39, 40) stitches, if necessary.

Knit every row until there are 5 (5, 6, 6) Garter Stitch ridges showing on the RS, end after knitting a RS row.

With WS facing, Cast Off knitwise. Cut yarn.

Divide for second Sleeve: Attach yarn and knit across 62 (70, 76, 82) stitches of Back to next marker; knit next 50 (54, 59, 64) stitches for sleeve, Turn.

Work as for first sleeve.

Finish Dividing Row: Attach yarn and knit remaining stitches of right Front to end of row. (134, 150, 162, 174 sts on circular needle for Body)

BODY

Next Row: (WS) K5, purl to last 5 stitches, K5.

Next Row: (WS) K5, purl to first sleeve junction, pick up 2 stitches to close gaps, purl to next sleeve junction, pick up 2 stitches, purl to last 5 stitches, K5.

Next Row: (RS) Knit to extra underarm stitches, K2tog, knit to extra underarm stitches, K2tog, knit to end of row. (136, 152, 164, 176 sts)

Next Row: K5, purl to last 5 stitches, K5.

Row 1: (RS) Knit.

Row 2: K5, purl to last 5 stitches, K5.

Repeat last 2 rows continuing to work button-holes every 9 (10, 10, 10) garter stitch ridges, until sweater measures 8½ (9½, 11½, 13½)"/21.5 (24, 29, 34.5) cm, ending after a WS row. You can lengthen the sweater here and work to 3½"/9 cm shy of desired length.

Work Border.

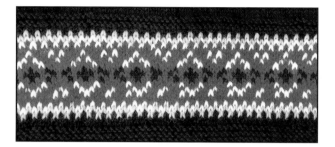

BORDER

Next Row: (RS) Continuing with MC, Knit.

Next Row: (WS) Knit. (makes a ridge)

Shaping Row: (RS) With MC, knit increasing or decreasing as indicated for your size — Size 1 increase 4 stitches (140 sts), Size 2 decrease 2 stitches (150 sts), Size 4 decrease 4 stitches (160 sts), Size 6 increase 4 stitches (180 sts).

Next Row: Knit. (makes a ridge)

Note: If you find your tension tightens up when working with a colour pattern, change to a size larger needle for the colour work, returning to the 4.0mm/US6 needle for the garter stitch ridges at the bottom of the sweater.

Work CHART A, working buttonbands in MC as set (you will have to wind a small bit of MC yarn for knitting the second buttonband or use the other end from the same ball of yarn for the duration of the Chart).

Decrease Row: With MC, K9, K2tog, *K8, K2tog; repeat across to last 9 stitches, K9.

Next Row: Knit.

Knit every row until 5 (5, 6, 6) ridges are showing on RS, ending after knitting a RS row.

With WS facing, **Cast Off** while knitting. Cut Yarn.

FINISHING

Sew sleeve seams if necessary, closing gap at underarm. Weave in ends.

Sew buttons over the buttonholes on the Left Band for girls or Right Band for boys.

Block if necessary.

CHART A - NAVY   CHART A - RED

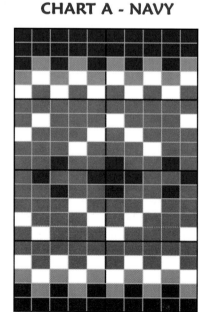
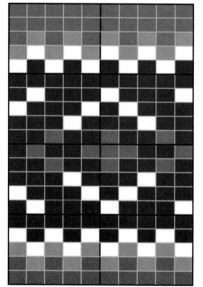

CHART A:

Starting with Row 1, read odd numbered rows (RS) from right to left and even rows (WS) from left to right.

PUFFY STRIPES

Experience Level: With Gusto!
(Enthusiastic Beginner)

adapted by Dana Gibbons

The Puffy Stripes was knit in Butterfly Super 10 cotton, Main Colour #3834 Tile Blue, accents Sunflower #3356, Purple Iris #3940 and Imperial Teal #3784 .

ABBREVIATIONS:

CC: Contrast Colour.

MC: Main Colour.

Inc 1: Increase 1 stitch. See Increases on page 16 for descriptions of various increase methods.

K2tog: Right slanting decrease. Knit the next two stitches together.

pm: Place a marker.

sm: Slip the marker.

st(s): Stitch(es).

SSK: Left leaning decrease. Slip the next stitch as if to knit, slip the next stitch as if to knit, insert the left needle into the fronts of the two slipped stitches on the right needle. Knit the 2 slipped stitches together.

yo: Yarn Over to make a hole (eyelet) and increase one stitch.

Cosy, fun, and a learning tool too?
A variation of the basic pullover that gives young wearers bright stripes to count. We like to involve them choosing colours too--it's hard to make a bad choice!

Needles:

5.0mm/US8 needle - Collar Cast On ONLY
4.0mm/US6 circular needle (40 cm/16" long)
Optional for two larger sizes:
4.0mm/US6 circular needle (60 cm/24" long)
1 set of 4.0mm/US6 double-point needles for the sleeves.

Socks Only Needles: 5 needle set of 3.25mm/US3 double-pointed needles

Sweater & Hat Tension:

22 stitches = 4"/10 cm on 4.0mm/US6 needle in stocking stitch or needle needed to obtain this tension.

Socks Only Tension:

24 stitches = 4"/10 cm on 3.25mm/US3 needle in stocking stitch or needle needed to obtain this tension.

Directions are given for size 1, other sizes are in brackets. If only one figure is shown, it applies to all sizes.

To Fit:	1 year	2 year	4 year	6 year
Chest Size of:	20"	22"	24"	26"
	51 cm	56 cm	61 cm	66 cm
Finished Size:				
Chest	24"	26"	28"	30"
	61 cm	66 cm	71 cm	76 cm
Sleeve Length	6½"	8"	10"	12"
	16.5 cm	20.5 cm	25.5 cm	30.5 cm
Body Length	12"	13"	15"	17"
	30.5 cm	33 cm	38 cm	43 cm
Hat	17½"	17½"	18"	19"
	44.5 cm	44.5 cm	46 cm	48 cm
Socks	4½"	5½"	6½"	7½"
	11.5 cm	14 cm	16.5 cm	19 cm

Materials: DK Yarn - 125g, 230m/249yds

Pullover:				
Main Colour	1	1¼	1½	2
Contrast Colour 1	½	½	1	1
Contrast Colour 2	¼	¼	½	½
Contrast Colour 3	¼	¼	½	½
Hat:				
Main Colour	¼	¼	½	½
Contrast Colours	¼	¼	¼	¼
Socks:				
Main Colour	¼	¼	¼	¼
Contrast Colours	odds	odds	odds	odds
Ring markers	4	4	4	4

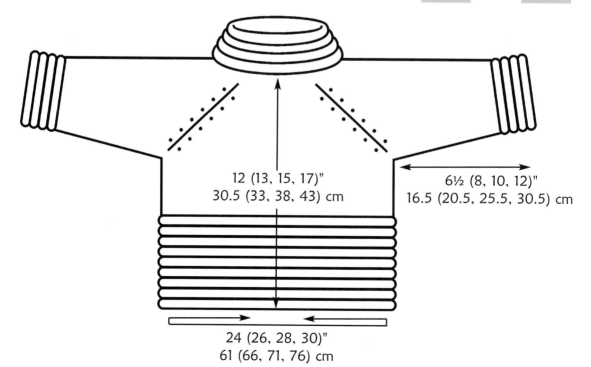

12 (13, 15, 17)"
30.5 (33, 38, 43) cm

6½ (8, 10, 12)"
16.5 (20.5, 25.5, 30.5) cm

24 (26, 28, 30)"
61 (66, 71, 76) cm

Puffy Stripes

Cast on with larger needle to ensure the sweater will go over your small person's head easily.

TO BEGIN

With 5.0mm/US8 needle and CC2 (CC2, CC1, CC1) , Cast On 72 (80, 88, 96) stitches.

Next Round: With smaller sized circular needle, purl the stitches off the larger needle.

Join in the round being careful not to twist your stitches. Place a marker to indicate the beginning of the round.

Purl 3 rounds.

Knit 1 round. Break Contrast Colour.

```
PUFFY STRIPE PATTERN:
Knit 1 round.
Purl 4 rounds.
Knit 1 round.
```

Work Puffy Stripe Pattern above with CC3 (CC3, CC2, CC2).

Sizes 4 and 6 ONLY: Work the Puffy Stripe Pattern again in CC3.

All Sizes: With CC1 work one more Puffy Stripe.

Reality Check: Sizes 1 & 2 should have 3 puffy stripes, and Sizes 4 and 6 should have 4 puffy stripes for the collar.

YOKE

Four shapelines are used to increase on the yoke. Each shapeline consists of 2 stitches. Every other round, increases are worked before and after each of the shapelines. In the next round you will place a marker in the centre of the 4 shapelines.

Note: Make the First Marker different in some way (a different colour or tie a piece of coloured yarn to it) so that you will know where each round begins.

Marker Round: With Main Colour, slip first marker, K1 (shapeline stitch), K26 (28, 30, 32) for the Body, K1 (shapeline stitch); place marker, K1 (shapeline stitch), K6 (8, 10, 12) for the sleeve, K1 (shapeline stitch); place marker, K1 (shapeline stitch), K26 (28, 30, 32) for the Body, K1 (shapeline stitch); place marker, K1 (shapeline stitch), K6 (8, 10, 12), K1 (shapeline stitch).

Note: Increases are indicated by "Inc 1". Use the method of your choice, see page 16. Dana used a yo increase in her sample.

Increase Round: *Slip marker, K1 (shapeline), Inc 1, knit to 1 stitch before next marker, Inc 1, K1; repeat from * around to First Marker.

Straight Round: Knit.

Repeat the last 2 rounds until you have 208 (232, 248, 264) stitches on your needle. Change to longer circular needle when needed.

Reality Check: There should be 62 (68, 72, 76) stitches between the Markers for both the Body sections (includes the shapeline stitches). The sleeves should have 42 (48, 52, 56) stitches between the Markers. If you don't have this exact number don't worry about it, but try to fudge the numbers so that both the Body sections have the same number of stitches between the Markers, and both the sleeves have the same number.

If Yoke is not yet 6 (7, 7½, 8)"/15 (18, 19, 20.5) cm (measure vertically from base of collar to needles), knit around without increases until you reach this length.

Divide Body and Sleeves: The Divide Round below will separate the sleeves and the body. The sleeve stitches will now be held on spare yarn as you work the Body first.

The Body stitches stay on the circular needle and stitches are cast on at the underarms.

At each shapeline, one shapeline stitch will go with the sleeve and one shapeline stitch with the Body stitches.

Divide Round: Remove markers as you go, *K62 (68, 72, 76) stitches to next marker — these are the Body stitches which stay on the circular needle; K42 (48, 52, 56) stitches to the next Marker and thread the 42 (48, 52, 56) stitches just knit, onto a spare piece of yarn for the sleeve (sleeve stitches plus one shapeline stitch before and after); repeat from * once more. (124, 136, 144, 152 sts on circular needle for the Body.)

BODY

Next Round: Place a marker for the beginning of the round, knit to underarm, Cast On 4 (4,

5, 7) stitches, knit to underarm, Cast On 4 (4, 5, 7) stitches.   (132, 144, 154, 166 sts)

Knit 1 round.

Work the Puffy Stripe Pattern with CC1, continue to repeat pattern with CC2, CC3, and then MC.

Repeat this colour sequence of puffy stripes until you have reached a desired length of 12 (13, 15, 17)"/30.5 (33, 38, 43) cm from the base of collar down to needle or desired length for the child you are making it for. On the last stripe end by working Round 6 as **Cast off** purlwise.

SLEEVES

Set-Up Round: With double-point needles and RS facing, starting in the centre of the underarm stitches, pick up and knit 2 (2, 3, 4) stitches from the cast on edge of underarm stitches, pick up an extra stitch here at the corner to help close the gap, knit the sleeve stitches on spare yarn, pick up an extra stitch here at the corner to help close the gap, pick up and knit 2 (2, 2, 3) stitches to centre of underarm, place marker.   (48, 54, 59, 65 sts)

Note: I don't think it is necessary to taper the sleeves for small children so I have put in directions for a straight sleeve for the 2 smallest sizes. However, with the instructions below you can taper the sleeves for all the sizes.

Straight sleeve (2 smaller sizes): Knit every round until sleeve measures 4½ (6)"/11.5 (15) cm or to 2"/5 cm shy of desired length for the recipient of the sweater. Now work the Cuff.

- OR -

Taper the Sleeves
Set-up Round (2 smaller sizes): Inc 1 stitch, knit to end of round.   (49, 55 sts)

All Sizes:

Knit 7 rounds.

Next and every 8th round: K1, SSK, knit to 2 stitches before the end of the round, K2tog.

Repeat the last 8 rounds (Do not decrease to less than 41, 41, 45, 45 stitches), until sleeve measures 4½ (6, 8, 10)"/11.5 (15, 20.5, 25.5) cm or to 2"/5 cm shy of desired length for a 3 stripe cuff or 2½"/6 cm for a 4 stripe cuff.

Now work the Cuff.

CUFF

Next Round (Straight Sleeve ONLY): K2tog, *K4 (2), K2tog; repeat from * 6 (12) more times, ending with K4 (0).   (40, 40 sts)

I created this version for my American cousins in Butterfly Super 10 cotton in Cobalt #3871, white & Scarlet #3997. Tie colours through the increase holes and add fun, colourful buttons.

- OR -

Next Round (Tapered Sleeve): Knit, decreasing to 40 (40, 44, 44) stitches.

All Sizes:

Four Stripes Cuff: Work Puffy Stripe Pattern with CC1, repeat with CC2, CC3 and with CC1 again ending this last stripe by working Round 6 as **Cast off** purlwise.

Three Stripes Cuff: Work Puffy Stripe Pattern with CC1, repeat with CC2, and with CC1 again ending this last stripe by working Round 6 as **Cast off** purlwise.

This sweater also lends itself to using small amounts of many colours. Use similar weights of yarn and any eye catching colourway that appeals.

SLOUCH SOCKS & PUFFY HAT

With such little socks, the "shortie" 5"/12.5 cm double-point needle sets are ideal. This pattern is written for a set of 5 double-pointed needles. You'll need to adjust the number of stitches on each needle if you are using a 4 needle set.

> **PUFFY STRIPE PATTERN:**
>
> Knit 1 round.
> Purl 4 rounds.
> Knit 1 round.

TO BEGIN SOCKS

With MC, and size 3.25mm/US3 double-point needles Cast On 36 (36, 40, 40) stitches loosely. (It's important to cast on loosely so the very top row of the sock has lots of give.) Divide stitches evenly onto four needles. Join in the round, being careful not to twist the stitches.

TOP OF SOCK

With MC, work (K2, P2) rib for 1"/2.5 cm.

Knit 1 round. Break yarn.

Work Puffy Stripe Pattern with CC1, repeat with CC2 and CC3.

Continue with Pattern in whatever colour you please, for 3½ (4, 4, 4½)"/9 (10, 10, 11.5) cm.

Knit 2 rounds with last colour used. Break yarn.

HEEL FLAP (worked in CC2 or colour of your choice)

This is the 'back' or flap of the sock heel.

Set-Up Heel: With selected colour, Knit 9 (9, 10, 10) stitches across the 1st needle. Turn work and on a single needle Sl1, P17 (17, 19, 19) stitches.

Reality Check: You now have 1 needle with 18 (18, 20, 20) stitches for the heel flap and 2 needles of 9 (9, 10, 10) each for the instep.

The two needles with 9 (9, 10, 10) sts each are held for the instep. You won't use these stitches until you complete the back of the heel.

Work back and forth on the 18 (18, 20, 20) stitches for the heel, starting with the Right Side facing as follows:

1st Row: (RS) *Sl1, K1; repeat from * to end of row, Turn.

2nd Row: Sl1, purl to the end of the row, Turn.

Repeat these two rows until heel flap measures 1¾ (1¾, 2, 2)"/4.5 (4.5, 5, 5) cm, ending after a WS row. Continue with same colour.

TURNING THE HEEL

Row 1: (RS) K9 (9, 10, 10) across to the centre of the heel, then knit 4 more stitches, SSK, TURN.

Row 2: Sl1, P8, P2tog, Turn.

Row 3: Sl1, K8, SSK, Turn.

Row 4: Sl1, P8, P2tog, Turn.

Repeat last 2 rows until all side stitches have been worked, ending after completing a WS row. (You should have 10 stitches left on the needle.)

Knit 5 stitches to the middle of the RS row.

Break yarn.

THE HEEL GUSSET (worked in MC)

Now that you're picking up stitches along the heel flap you are back to using 4 needles and knitting with the 5th.

Set-Up Round: Using a new needle and MC, knit next 5 stitches and with the same needle, pick up and K9 (10, 11, 11) stitches along the right side of heel; knit across instep stitches (keeping them on the two needles); then with the 5th needle, pick up and K9 (10, 11, 11) stitches along left side of heel and work across the remaining 5 heel stitches.

Reality Check: You should have 14 (15, 16, 16) stitches on the 1st needle, the 2nd and 3rd needles should each have 9 (9, 10, 10) instep stitches, and the 4th should have 14 (15, 16, 16) stitches. If not, adjust your stitches to achieve this.

The rounds now begins at the centre back of the heel.

SHAPE THE GUSSET (worked in MC)

Round 1: Knit to last 3 stitches on the 1st needle, K2tog, K1; knit across both the 2nd and 3rd needles (instep stitches); at the beginning of the 4th needle, K1, SSK, knit to end.

Round 2: Knit.

Repeat these two rounds, decreasing at the end of the 1st needle and the beginning of the 4th needle, until you have a total of 36 (36, 40, 40) stitches.

Knit every round on these stitches until the foot measures approximately 2 (3, 4, 5)"/5 (7.5, 10, 12.5) cm from beginning of heel gusset.

Break yarn.

SHAPE THE TOE (worked in CC2 or colour of your choice)

Change to CC2 or colour of your choice, Knit 1 round.

Round 1: With selected colour, Knit to last 3 stitches on the 1st needle, K2tog, K1; at the beginning of the 2nd needle K1, SSK, knit to end of needle; knit to last 3 stitches on the 3rd needle and K2tog, K1; on the 4th needle K1, SSK, knit to end of needle. (32, 32, 36, 36 sts)

Round 2: Knit.

Repeat these two rounds until 20 stitches remain.

Repeat Round 1 only, until 8 stitches remain. Cut yarn, leaving an 8"/20.5 cm tail.

Thread the end of the yarn onto a blunt sewing needle and pass the yarn through all the remaining stitches; pull them tight and secure.

Sew in the ends and you're done!

PUFFY STRIPE HAT

Starting from the TOP using 2 size 4.0mm/US6 double-pointed needles, leave a 5"/13 cm tail and with CC1, Cast On 4 stitches.

Work I-Cord for 1½"/4 cm (see page 102). Cut CC1.

Leave these stitches on one of the dp needles.

Repeat I-Cord above with CC2 and CC3.

You will have 3 I-Cord tails, each left on a dp needle.

Join up I-Cords: With MC and dp needle, knit 4 stitches from needle with CC1 stitches on it, with another dp needle, knit 4 stitches of CC2, with third dp needle, knit 4 stitches of CC3. (12 sts)

Place marker for beginning of round, and join in the round being careful not to twist the stitches.

Next Round: Knit.

Next Round: [K3, Inc 1 stitch using Backward Loop] 4 times. (16 sts) See page 16 for Backward Loop instructions.

WHEEL OF HAT

The wheel of the hat has 8 sections. You will be increasing 8 stitches every second round.

Change to circular needle when you can.

Next Round: Continuing with MC, Knit.

Increase Round: *K2, M1; repeat from * to end of round. (24 sts)

Next Round: Knit.

Increase Round: *K3, M1; repeat from * to end of round. (32 sts)

Next Round: Knit.

Increase Round: *K4, M1; repeat from * to end of round.

Next Round: Knit.

Continue increasing at the end of each of the 8 sections every second round until you have a total of 96 (96, 96, 104) stitches. (12, 12, 12, 13 sts in each of the 8 sections)

Next Round: Knit, increasing 0 (0, 0, 4) stitches evenly across the round. (96, 96, 100, 104 sts)

BODY OF HAT

Work the Puffy Stripe Pattern in the following colour sequences:

PUFFY STRIPE PATTERN:

Knit 1 round.
Purl 4 rounds.
Knit 1 round.

Size 1 & 2: Work Puffy Stripe Pattern with CC1, repeat with CC2, CC3 and work last stripe with CC1. (4 puffy stripes in Body of hat.)

Size 3: Work Puffy Stripe Pattern with CC1, repeat for CC2, CC3, CC2, CC3, and work last stripe with CC1. (6 puffy stripes in Body of hat.)

Size 4: Work Puffy Stripe Pattern with CC1, repeat with CC2, CC3, MC, CC3, CC2, and work last stripe with CC1. (7 puffy stripes in Body of hat.)

All Sizes:

Next Round: With MC, knit.

Next Round: With MC, purl.

Work (K1, P1) rib for 1"/2.5 cm or desired length of hat.

Cast Off in rib with 4.5mm/US7 needle for a looser edge.

FINISH

Make I-Cord bobbles: Fold the I-Cord in half away from the centre of the crown of the hat and using the 5"/13 cm tail secure the bobble at the base of the I-Cord and sew in the end. **Repeat** with the other I-Cords.

Sew in ends.

MEGAN'S RUFFLE

Experience Level: Intermediate

adapted by Megan Lacey

ABBREVIATIONS:

Inc 1: Increase 1 stitch in the next stitch. See Increases on page 16 for descriptions of various increase methods.

K2tog: Right slanting decrease. Knit the next two stitches together.

Kfb: Increase by knitting into the front and back of a stitch.

pm: Place a marker.

PSSO: Pass slipped stitch over.

sm: Slip the marker.

SSK: Left leaning decrease. Slip the next stitch as if to knit, slip the next stitch as if to knit, insert the left needle into the fronts of the two slipped stitches on the right needle. Knit the 2 slipped stitches together.

st(s): Stitch(es).

yo: Yarn Over to make a hole (eyelet) and increase one stitch.

Knit it up brightly (as on our cover) or in subtle tones--either way it's a girly and cute adaptation of the basic pullover that your little fashionplate will love.

Needles:

5.0mm/US8 needle - Collar Cast On ONLY

4.0mm/US6 circular needle (40 cm/16" long)

4.0mm/US6 circular needle (60 cm/24" long)

1 set of 4.0mm/US6 double-point needles for the sleeves.

Tension:

22 stitches = 4"/10 cm on 4.0mm/US6 needle in stocking stitch or needle needed to obtain this tension.

Directions are given for size 1, other sizes are in brackets. If only one figure is shown, it applies to all sizes.

To Fit:	1 year	2 year	4 year	6 year
Chest Size of:	20"	22"	24"	26"
	51 cm	56 cm	61 cm	66 cm
Finished Size:				
Chest	24"	26"	28"	30"
	61 cm	66 cm	71 cm	76 cm
Sleeve Length	6½"	8"	10"	12"
	16.5 cm	20.5 cm	25.5 cm	30.5 cm
Body Length	12"	13"	15"	17"
	30.5 cm	33 cm	38 cm	43 cm

Materials: DK Yarn - 50g ball, 100m/109yds

Main Colour	4	5	6	7
Contrast Colour 1	1	2	2	2
Contrast Colour 2	1	1	1	1
Contrast Colour 3	1	1	1	1
Ring markers	4	4	4	4

Sample, left, is knit in Dale Heilo in Main Colour #4845, CC1 #9335, CC2 #2931 and CC3 #3046.

CHART B

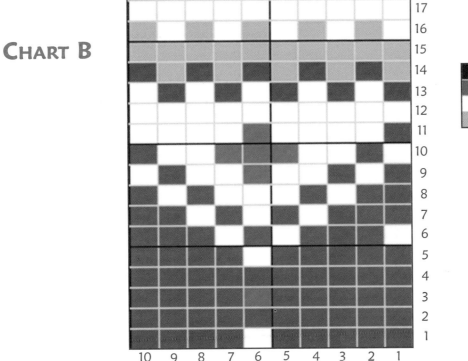

Main Colour
Contrast Colour 1
Contrast Colour 2
Contrast Colour 3

The lace collar is incorporated into this design and not knit separately and sewn on later!

Cast on with the largest needle (collar cast on ONLY) to ensure the sweater will go over your small person's head easily. Knit the collar with the 4.0mm/US6 needle.

TO BEGIN

With Contrast Colour 1 and 5.0mm/US8 needle **Cast On** 72 (80, 88, 96) stitches.

CHART A

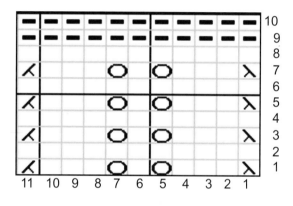

Knit
Purl
Sl1, K1, PSSO
Yarn Over
K2tog

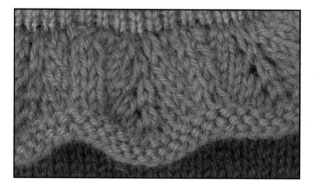

Next Round: With shorter 4.0mm/US6 circular needle, knit the stitches off the larger needle.

Join in the round being careful not to twist your stitches. Place marker (pm) to indicate the beginning of the round.

Knit every round for 1½ (1½, 2, 2)"/4 (4, 5, 5) cm. Break CC1.

LACE RUFFLE

Next Round: With CC3 and 4.0mm/US6 shorter circular needle, Knit.

Increase Round: With CC3, knit, increasing evenly around to 143 (154, 176, 187) stitches. (Megan used a kfb increase.)

Work Chart A.

Cast off knitwise, break CC3 and sew in end.

Join MC to base of the rolled collar: With the WS facing, pick up and knit one stitch for each stitch around base of CC1 collar. (72, 80, 88, 96 sts)

YOKE

Four shapelines are used to increase on the yoke. Each shapeline consists of 2 stitches with a marker in the centre of these 2 stitches. Every other round, increases are worked before and after each shapelines.

In the next round you will place a marker in the centre of the 4 shapelines.

Note: Make each of the First Marker different in some way (a different colour or tie a piece of coloured yarn to it) so that you will know where each round begins.

Marker Round: Slip First Marker, K1 (shapeline stitch), K26 (28, 30, 32) for the Body, K1 (shapeline stitch); pm, K1 (shapeline stitch), K6 (8, 10, 12) for the sleeve, K1 (shapeline stitch); pm, K1 (shapeline stitch), K26 (28, 30, 32) for the Body, K1 (shapeline stitch); pm, K1 (shapeline stitch), K6 (8, 10, 12), K1 (shapeline stitch).

This sample was knit using Butterfly Super 10 Cotton in colours Kelly Green #3764, Daffodil #3553, Light Mauve #3936 and Purple Iris #3940.

The Russian Hat was knit using Stylecraft Eskimo DK Eyelash in Purple #5244 and Emu Superwash in Violet #3633. The pattern for the Russian Hat is on page 33.

*Note: Increases are indicated by "Inc 1". Use the method of your choice, see Increases on page 16. Megan used a **yo** increase.*

Increase Round: *Slip marker, K1 (shapeline), Inc 1 stitch, knit to 1 stitch before next marker, Inc 1 stitch, K1; repeat from * around to First Marker.

Straight Round: Knit.

Repeat the last 2 rounds until you have 208 (232, 248, 264) stitches on your needle.

Note: Change to longer 4.0mm/US6 circular needle when the increased number of sts become too many for the shorter needle.

Reality Check: There should be 62 (68, 72, 76) stitches between the Markers for both the Body sections (includes the shapeline stitches). The sleeves should have 42(48, 52, 56) stitches between the Markers. If you don't have this exact number don't worry about it, but try to fudge the numbers so that both the Body sections have the same number of stitches between the Markers, and both the sleeves have the same number.

If the Yoke is not yet 6 (7, 7½, 8)"/15 (18, 19, 20.5) cm deep, measuring vertically down the centre Back from the base of the collar down to your needle, continue to knit every round without any more increases until you have reached the length above.

DIVIDE BODY AND SLEEVES

The Divide Round below will separate the sleeves and the body. The sleeve stitches will now be held on spare yarn as you work the Body first.

The Body stitches stay on the circular needle and stitches are cast on at the underarms.

At each shapeline, one shapeline stitch will go with the sleeve and one shapeline stitch with the Body stitches.

Divide Round: Remove markers as you go, *Knit to next marker (62, 68, 72, 76 stitches — these are the Body stitches which stay on the circular needle); K42 (48, 52, 56 stitches) to the next Marker and thread the 42 (48, 52, 56) stitches just knit, onto a spare piece of yarn for the sleeve (sleeve stitches plus one shapeline stitch before and after); repeat from * once more.   (124, 136, 144, 152 sts on circular needle for the Body.)

BODY

Next Round: Knit to underarm, Cast On 4 (4, 5, 7) stitches, knit to underarm, Cast On 2 (2, 2, 3) stitches, place marker in centre of underarm for beginning of round, Cast On 2 (2, 3, 4) more stitches.   (132, 144, 154, 166 sts)

Next Round: Knit around the Body to underarm marker.

Knit every round until the sweater measures 7 (8, 10, 13)"/18 (20.5, 25.5, 33) cm from the base of collar down to needle.

Next Round: Knit, increasing 8 (6, 6, 4) stitches evenly around body. (140, 150, 160, 170 sts.)

Work Chart B.

Next Round: With CC1, Knit around, decreasing 10 stitches evenly around the Body.

Knit every round for 2½"/6.5 cm. (The extra ½"/1.5 cm is for the rolled edge.)

Cast Off.

SLEEVES

Set-Up Round: With double-point needles and RS facing, starting in the centre of the underarm stitches, pick up and knit 2 (2, 3, 4) stitches from the cast on edge of underarm stitches, pick up an extra stitch here at the corner to help close the gap, knit the sleeve stitches on spare yarn, pick up an extra stitch here at the corner to help close the gap, pick up and knit 2 (2, 2, 3) stitches to centre of underarm, place marker.   (48, 54, 59, 65 sts)

Note: I don't think it is necessary to taper the sleeves for small children so I have put in directions for a straight sleeve for the 2 smallest sizes. However, with the instructions below you can taper the sleeves for all the sizes.

Straight sleeve: (2 smaller sizes) Knit every round until sleeve measures 4½ (6)"/11.5 (15) cm from underarm or to 2"/5 cm shy of desired length for the recipient of the sweater. Now work the Cuff.

- OR -

Taper the Sleeves:
Set-Up Round: (2 smaller sizes) Inc 1 stitch, knit to end of round. (49, 55 stitches) The increased stitch becomes the underarm seamline stitch.

(ALL SIZES) Knit 7 rounds.

Next and every 8th round: K1, SSK, knit to 2 stitches before the end of the round, K2tog.

Repeat the last 8 rounds (Do Not decrease to less than 41, 41, 45, 45 stitches), until sleeve measures 4½ (6, 8, 9)"/11.5 (15, 20, 23) cm from the underarm or to 2"/5 cm shy of desired length for the recipient of the sweater. Now work the Cuff.

CUFF

Next Round (Straight Sleeve — 2 smaller sizes): K2tog, *K4 (2), K2tog; repeat from * 6 (12) more times, ending with K4 (0). (40, 40 sts)

Next Round (Tapered Sleeve): Knit, decreasing to 40 (40, 44, 44) sts.

With CC1, Knit every round for 2½"/6.5 cm. (The extra ½"/1.5 cm is for the rolled edge.)

Cast Off.

Sew in ends so that they can not be seen when the edges roll.

DANCING PRINCESS

Experience Level: Intermediate

adapted by Maureen Mason-Jamieson

NOTE FROM MAUREEN:

I used 2 balls of the fingering weight glitter yarn held together to bring it up to DK weight. If you can find a DK weight glitter yarn then only use a single strand but the same yardage.

ABBREVIATIONS:

Inc 1: Increase 1 stitch. See Increases on page 16 for descriptions of various increase methods.

K2tog: Right slanting decrease. Knit the next two stitches together.

pm: Place a marker.

sm: Slip the marker.

SSK: Left leaning decrease. Slip the next stitch as if to knit, slip the next stitch as if to knit, insert the left needle into the fronts of the two slipped stitches on the right needle. Knit the 2 slipped stitches together.

st(s): Stitch(es).

yo: Yarn Over to make a hole (eyelet) and increase one stitch.

Let the pirouettes begin! Your little balle-rina or jazz dancing mini diva will keep these glittery tassels bouncing, and you'll enjoy how easy Maureen has made it to add style and sparkle to the basic pullover.

Needles:

5.0mm/US8 needle - Collar Cast On ONLY
4.0mm/US6 circular needle (40 cm/16" long)
Optional for two larger sizes:
4.0mm/US6 circular needle (60 cm/24" long)
1 set of 4.0mm/US6 double-point needles for the sleeves.
Optional for crochet cord (cord can also be made knitting I-cord): 4.0mm/US6 crochet hook

Tension:

22 stitches = 4"/10 cm on 4.0mm/US6 needle in stocking stitch or needle needed to obtain this tension.

Directions are given for size 1, other sizes are in brackets. If only one figure is shown, it applies to all sizes.

To make a tassel: Cut a 10"/25 cm length of CC yarn and set aside. Wind CC around a 2½"/7 cm piece of cardboard 20 times. Slip 10"/25 cm length under all strands at upper edge of cardboard. Draw 3"/7.5 cm through, knot securely near strands. Cut yarn loops at lower edge of the cardboard. Wrap remaining 7"/18 cm tightly six times around loops ½"/1 cm below top knot to form tassel neck. Thread the end into tapestry needle and draw end under tassel neck and into topknot. Trim all the ends neatly.

To attach five tassels to sweater: Cut a 2 yard/ 183 cm length of CC yarn and thread it through a tapestry needle. Working from right to left eyelet column, anchor yarn end in CC hem roll just below first eyelet column. *Weave yarn upward in and out of eyelets, coming out at the top hole. Insert yarn into the tassel topknot and pull through securing tassel to sweater. Re-trace your woven path back down to the base of the eyelet column. Neatly weave your yarn along the top of the hem roll to the base of the next eyelet column. Repeat from *. When you have completed attaching tassels, anchor yarn end in CC hem roll just below last eyelet column.

To Fit:	1 year	2 year	4 year	6 year
Chest Size of:	20"	22"	24"	26"
	51 cm	56 cm	61 cm	66 cm
Finished Size:				
Chest	24"	26"	28"	30"
	61 cm	66 cm	71 cm	76 cm
Sleeve Length	6½"	8"	10"	12"
	16.5 cm	20.5 cm	25.5 cm	30.5 cm
Body Length	12"	13"	15"	17"
	30.5 cm	33 cm	38 cm	43 cm
Hat	17½	17½	18"	19"
	44.5 cm	44.5 cm	46 cm	48 cm

Materials: DK Yarn - 50g ball, 123m/135yds
Glitter Fingering yarn, 185m/202yds

Sweater:				
Main Colour	4	4	5	6
Contrast Colour	1	1	1	1
Hat:				
Main Colour	1	1	1	1
Contrast Colour	1	1	1	1
Ring markers	4	4	4	4

Both the sweater and the hat are knit in Naturally Magic Garden Tinsel #125 and the glitter yarn is Ironstone Yarns, Paris Nights.

A simple sweater and hat set with terrific glitter details to delight your little princess.

Dancing Princess options: Make each tassel a different colour for a rainbow princess. Make green tassel "palm trees" and attach them with brown Contrast Colour for a hula princess. For a more sedate princess, make sweater/hat in Main Colour with same colour tassels.

*Construction Note: The sample used a **yo** increase.*

TO BEGIN

Cast On with Contrast Colour and follow The Basic Pullover pattern as set to the YOKE. Break yarn.

With MC continue with The Basic Pullover pattern to the BODY section, ending after the Divide Round. (124, 136, 144, 152 sts on circular needle for BODY).

BODY

Next Round: Place a marker for the beginning of the round, knit to the first underarm, Cast On 4 (4, 5, 7) stitches, knit to the second underarm, Cast On 4 (4, 5, 7) stitches. (132, 144, 154, 166 sts)

Knit every round until the sweater measures 6 (7, 9, 11)"/ 15 (18, 23, 28) cm measuring from the base of the collar down to needle (collar is not included in this measurement) OR 6"/15 cm shy of desired length for the child you are making it for.

FOR SIZES 4 & 6 ONLY:

Next Round: K38 (41), Inc 1 stitch, K78 (84), Inc 1 stitch, knit to the end of the round. (156, 168) sts.

Reality Check: The total number of stitches on needle are 132 (144, 156, 168) sts.

To Place Eyelets across the Front:

Round 1: K10 (11, 12, 13), [K2tog, yo, K20 (22, 24, 26)] twice, K2tog, yo, K10 (11, 12, 13), knit across the Back to the end of the round.

Round 2: Knit.

Repeat Rounds 1 and 2, 3 more times (makes 3 vertical columns with 4 eyelet holes in each column).

Add additional Eyelet columns: (5 vertical columns of eyelet holes)

Round 3: K10 (11, 12, 13), [K2tog, yo, K9 (10, 11, 12)] 4 times, K2tog, yo, K10, (11, 12, 13), knit across the Back to the end of the round.

Round 4: Knit.

Repeat Rounds 3 and 4 until the sweater measures 10 (11, 13, 15)"/ 25.5 (28, 33, 38) cm from the base of collar down to the needle or 2"/5 cm shy of desired length for the child you are making it for, ending after a Round 3.

Decrease Round: *K5 (5, 6, 6), K2tog, [K9 (10, 11, 12), K2tog] 4 times, K8 (9, 11, 12), K2tog, K5 (5, 5, 6); repeat once more.

Next Round: K9 (10, 11, 12), [K2tog, yo, K8 (9, 10, 11)] 4 times, K2tog, yo K9 (10, 11, 12), knit to the end of the round.

Next Round: Knit.

Repeat the last 2 rounds, maintaining eyelet placement, for an additional 1½"/4 cm. Cut MC.

Change to Contrast Colour.

Knit every round for 1"/2.5 cm for hem roll. **Cast off.**

SLEEVES

Follow the Basic Pattern as follows:

For Sizes 1 & 2: Make the straight sleeve option.

For Sizes 4 & 6: Make the tapered sleeve.

All Sizes: Knit until the sleeve measures 4 (6, 8, 10)"/10 (15, 20.5, 25.5) cm or 3"/7.5 cm shy of desired length for the recipient of the sweater.

Now work the Cuff.

CUFF

Next Round (Straight Sleeve - Sizes 1 & 2): K2tog, *K4 (2), K2tog; repeat 6 (12) times, ending with K4 (0). (40, 40 sts).

- OR -

Next round (Tapered Sleeve - Sizes 4 & 6): Knit, decreasing to 44 stitches.

All Sizes - Place Eyelets across sleeve:

Round 1: K3, [K2tog, yo, K6 (6, 7, 7)] 4 times, K2tog, yo, K3.

Round 2: Knit.

Repeat Round 1 and 2, 6 more times -- five vertical columns of seven eyelet holes each. Cut Main Colour.

Change to Contrast Colour.

Knit every round for 1"/2.5 cm for hem roll.

Cast off.

TO FINISH

Make 15 tassels. Attach tassels, five tassels to each sleeve and 5 tassels on the Front of the sweater, following instructions. Weave in all remaining yarn ends. Weave in ends. Block sweater.

Place sweater on one princess and watch her dance with delight!

HAT

Make 4 Cords: Two options for working the cords are available for you to choose from. See page 102 for I-Cord instructions.

CROWN

Join up 4 cords: Using 2 double-point needles, with Contrast Colour, work a 4-stitch I-cord for 2 rounds. Cut Contrast Colour.

Change to Main Colour.

Work 1 round of a 4-stitch I-cord. Redistribute the stitches onto two double-point needles and using a third needle to knit.

Follow directions for Basic Top Down Rolled Brim Hat, with MC work increases for Crown until you have 96 stitches. Maureen's sample used the Backward Loop increase.

BODY OF HAT

Next Increase Round: Knit, increasing 0 (0, 4, 8) stitches evenly across round. (96, 96, 100, 104 sts)

Knit every round for 3 (3¼, 3½, 4)"/7.5 (8.5, 9, 10) cm. Cut MC.

Change to Contrast Colour.

Knit every round for 1"/2.5 cm. Fasten off.

TO FINISH

Thread short CC yarn tails at the hat crown through a tapestry needle and draw through 4-stitch I-cord to inside of hat. Wind the 10"/25 cm yarn end tightly around the base of the 4 Cords on the outside of the hat several times, to strengthen and neaten join and then thread the end through tapestry needle and draw through I-cord to inside of hat. Knot all yarn ends securely and trim.

Make 4 CC tassels as directed (see box) and attach to chain ends of hat. Block hat, place on one small child, ask them (politely, please!) to spin around.

CORD OPTIONS

Crochet Hook Option: *With 4.0mm/US6 crochet hook and CC, chain 14. Cut yarn leaving 4"/10 cm tail but do not fasten off. Place the remaining chain loop onto one 4.0mm/US6 double-pointed needle. Repeat from * two more times, leaving 10"/25 cm tail on third chain loop. Make a fourth cord of 14 chains, do not cut CC, use CC to continue with hat. Place remaining chain loop on double-pointed needle.

Reality Check: You will have four stitches on double-pointed needle.

I-Cord Option: If you prefer, make four 2-stitch I-cords, each 3"/7.5 cm long, on final round of each cord, decrease to 1 stitch and place this stitch on double-pointed needle as directed above. Break the yarn leaving a 3"/7.5 cm tail on the first two I-Cords. On the third I-Cord leave a 10"/25 cm tail. On the fourth I-Cord do not break the yarn, use CC to continue hat.

Reality Check: You will have four stitches on double-pointed needle.

THE PONCHO

Experience Level: With Gusto!
(Enthusiastic Beginner)

designed by Deb Gemmell

Needles:

5.0mm/US8 needle - Collar Cast On ONLY
4.0mm/US6 circular needle (40 cm/16" long)
Optional for two larger sizes:
4.0mm/US6 circular needle (60 cm/24" long)

Tension:

22 stitches = 4"/10 cm on 4.0mm/US6 needle in stocking stitch or needle needed to obtain this tension.

ABBREVIATIONS:

Inc 1: Increase 1 stitch. See Increases on page 16 for descriptions of various increase methods.

pm: Place a marker.

sm: Slip the marker.

To Fit:	1 year	2 year	4 year	6 year
Chest Size of:	20"	22"	24"	26"
	51 cm	56 cm	61 cm	66 cm
Finished Size:				
Chest	24"	26"	28"	30"
	61 cm	66 cm	71 cm	76 cm
Body Length	12"	13"	15"	17"
	30.5 cm	33 cm	38 cm	43 cm

Materials: DK Yarn -125g, 230m/250yds

Main Colour	2	2	3	3
Ring markers	4	4	4	4

Directions are given for size 1, other sizes are in brackets. If only one figure is shown, it applies to all sizes.

BEGIN AT THE COLLAR

With 5.0mm/US8 needle Cast On 72 (80, 88, 96) stitches.

With the smaller needle, work the stitches off the larger needle as follows:

Marker Round: *Place marker, (K1, P1) 14 (15, 16, 17) times, K1, place marker, (K1, P1) 3 (4, 5, 6) times, K1; repeat from * once more.

Note: Make the First Marker different in some way (a different colour or tie a piece of coloured yarn to it) so that you will know where each round begins.

Note: The two knit stitches with the marker in the centre will run down into the poncho body to become the shapelines for the increasing. (See photograph.)

Join in the round being careful not to twist your stitches.

Work rib as set for 1½ (1½, 2, 2)"/4 (4, 5, 5) cm.

YOKE

Four shapelines are used to increase on the yoke. Each shapeline consists of 2 stitches. Every other round, increases are worked before and after each of the shapelines. A marker is already in place in the centre of the 4 shapelines.

Change to longer circular needle when needed.

Note: Increases are indicated by "Inc 1 st". The increase used in sample was an Open M1.

Increase Round: *Slip marker, K1 (shapeline stitch), Inc 1 st, knit to 1 stitch before next marker, Inc 1 st, K1 (shapeline stitch); repeat from * around to First Marker.

Pattern Round: *Sm, K1, (K1, P1) to 2 stitches before marker, K2; repeat from * at next 3 markers.

Increase Round: *Sm, K1 (shapeline), Inc 1 stitch, knit to 1 stitch before next marker, Inc 1 st, K1 (shapeline stitch); repeat from * around to First Marker.

Straight Round: Knit.

Repeat the last 4 rounds until the poncho measures 10 (11, 13, 15)"/25.5 (28, 33, 38) cm from the bottom of collar down to needle (measure along the shapeline diagonal) or 2"/5 cm shy of desired length for the child you are making it for, *ending with a Pattern Round*.

RIB BORDER

Round 1: *Sm, K1, Inc 1 st, (K1, P1) to 2 stitches before next marker, K1, Inc 1 st, K1; repeat from * at next 3 markers.

Round 2: Sm, (K1, P1) to 1 stitch before marker, K1; repeat from * at next 3 markers.

Round 3: *Sm, K1, Inc 1 st, P1, (K1, P1) to 1 stitch before next marker, Inc 1 st, K1; repeat from * to end of round.

Round 4: *Sm, K1, (K1, P1) to 2 stitches before marker, K2; repeat from * to end of round.

Repeat last 4 rounds for 1½"/7.5 cm.

PICOT CORNERS

Cast Off Round: Remove marker, *Cast off in rib to next marker, remove marker, work Picot bump; repeat from * to end of round ending with a picot bump.

Picot bump on corners: Slip the stitch remaining on the right needle back onto the left needle, cast on 2 stitches onto left needle, cast off these 2 stitches.

OPTIONS

The picot bumps at the ends of the diagonal shapelines are fine as they are, but for the older child's sizes, they do lend themselves to becoming a post from which to attach tassels or bells or anything you might fancy to make this poncho your own creation.

For instructions on making tassels see page 103.

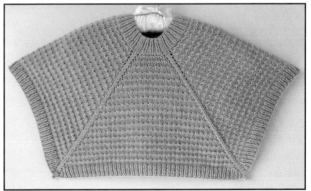

The poncho above was knit in Shelridge Farm's Soft Touch W4 in Apple Green; the poncho left was knit in Butterfly Super 10 Cotton in Dynastic Purple #3944.

PaintBox Jacket

Experience Level: With Gusto!
(Enthusiastic Beginner)

adapted by Lynda Gemmell

ABBREVIATIONS:

Inc 1: Increase 1 stitch. See Increases on page 16 for descriptions of various increase methods.

K2tog: Right slanting decrease. Knit the next two stitches together.

Kfb: Increase of 1 stitch also known as knitting into the front and back of a stitch. Knit into the front of the next stitch as usual and without taking the stitch off the left needle, knit into the back of the same stitch.

pm: Place a marker.

sm: Slip the marker.

SSK: Left leaning decrease. Slip the next stitch as if to knit, slip the next stitch as if to knit, insert the left needle into the fronts of the two slipped stitches on the right needle. Knit the 2 slipped stitches together.

yo: Yarn over to make a hole (eyelet) and increase one stitch. Bring wool under the right needle and forward to the front of your work, swing the wool over the right needle to the back of your work ready to work the next stitch. The resulting loop is purled in the next row.

I like the look of simple sweaters with multiple colours. The wilder the better. But if you have a conservative child, you can still use tone-on-tone colours for an interesting effect.

Just for fun, I made this jacket a cropped version without buttons and used a clasp closure. You can lengthen the body and/or include buttonholes by following the Body section of The Basic Cardigan pattern.

I used the **yo** increase in my sample.

Note: When working with blocks of colour it is important to twist the colours on the Wrong Side of the sweater. Pick up the new colour from under the old colour as you change from one colour to another. This will ensure that no holes result at the change point.

TO BEGIN

Follow The Basic Cardigan pattern with the changes indicated below.

Work the collar in C1 and add in the 5 body colours when you begin the **YOKE** as follows:

Row 1: (RS) **With C1**, Cast On 5 stitches (for left button band), knit these 5 stitches, place marker (pm), **with C2**, K10 (12, 13, 14) stitches for left Front, yo, K1, pm, **with C3**, K1, yo, K8 (8, 9, 10) stitches for sleeve, yo, K1, pm, **with C4**, K1, yo, K20 (24, 26, 28) stitches for Back, yo, K1, pm, **with C5**, K1, yo, K8 (8, 9, 10) stitches for sleeve, yo, K1, pm, **with C6**, K1, yo, K10 (12, 13, 14) stitches for right Front.

Row 2: **With C1**, Cast on 5 stitches (right button band), knit these 5 stitches, pm, *change to next colour, twisting colours and purl to next marker purling loops of yo increase; repeat from * to the last marker, change to C1, K5. (82, 90, 96, 102 sts)

Continue with The Basic Cardigan pattern changing colours as appropriate.

You can follow the instructions for buttonholes or you can use clasps as I have which do not require buttonholes.

Work the sleeve cuffs in C1.

Work the Body until the sweater measures 8 (9, 11, 13)"/ 20.5 (23, 28, 33) cm (measuring from the first row of the back colour) for a

To Fit:	1 year	2 year	4 year	6 year
Chest Size of:	20"	22"	24"	26"
	51 cm	56 cm	61 cm	66 cm
Finished Size:				
Chest	24"	26"	28"	30"
	61 cm	66 cm	71 cm	76 cm
Sleeve Length	6½"	8"	10"	12"
	16.5 cm	20.5 cm	25.5 cm	30.5 cm
Body Length	9"	10"	12"	14"
	23 cm	25.5 cm	305 cm	35.5 cm

Materials: DK Yarn -50g, 123m/135yds

C1 (collar, cuffs)	1	1	1	1
C2 (left front)	1	1	1	1
C3 (sleeve)	1	1	1	1
C4 (back)	1	1	2	2
C5 (sleeve)	1	1	1	1
C6 (right front)	1	1	1	1
Ring markers	6	6	6	6

Clasps as appropriate

Above is a picture of the sweater showing the colour twisted at the colour changes.

The PaintBox Jacket was knit in Naturally, Magic Garden Buttons in colours navy #879, yellow #877, purple #886, red #875, turquoise 887 and the back was done in jade #878.

short jacket. Feel free to knit the Body to the length you want!

Then finish by working the Garter Stitch Border in C1.

CLASSIC CABLE

Experience Level: Intermediate

adapted by Lynda Gemmell

ABBREVIATIONS:

Backward Loop Increase: Make an increase by putting a backward loop of yarn on the right-hand needle. It will be worked as a stitch in the next round.

Inc 1: Increase 1 stitch. See Increases on page 16 for descriptions of various increase methods.

pm: Place a marker.

sm: Slip the marker.

K2tog: Right slanting decrease. Knit the next two stitches together.

SSK: Left leaning decrease. Slip the next stitch as if to knit, slip the next stitch as if to knit, insert the left needle into the fronts of the two slipped stitches on the right needle. Knit the 2 slipped stitches together.

Cables are shown to their best advantage when knit with smooth, tightly twisted yarn. Light colours show the stitches better than dark colours (and are easier to work with). A firm wool or cotton yarn works well.

Needles:

4.5mm/US7 circular needle (16"/40 cm long) for Cast On and Cast Off ONLY

4.0mm/US6 circular needle (16"/40 cm long)

4.0mm/US6 circular needle (24"/60 cm long)

4.0mm/US6 double-point needles (for "no sew" sleeves & hat)

Cable needle

Tension:

22 stitches = 4"/10 cm on 4.0mm/US6 needle in stocking stitch or needle needed to obtain this tension.

To Fit:	1 year	2 year	4 year	6 year
Chest Size of:	20"	22"	24"	26"
	51 cm	56 cm	61 cm	66 cm
Finished Size:				
Chest	24"	26"	28"	30"
	61 cm	66 cm	71 cm	76 cm
Sleeve Length	6½"	8"	10"	12"
	16.5 cm	20.5 cm	25.5 cm	30.5 cm
Body Length	12"	13"	15"	17"
	30.5 cm	33 cm	38 cm	43 cm

Materials: DK Yarn - 50g ball, 119m /130yds

Pullover	4	5	6	7
Hat 17"/19"	1		1	
Ring markers	8	8	8	8

Directions are given for size 1, other sizes are in brackets. If only one figure is shown, it applies to all sizes.

The Classic Cable Sweater and Hat were knit with Stylecraft Emu Superwash wool in Cream.

Cables tend to pull in the width of a garment and to take more yarn than you might expect for a sweater this size, so please ensure you have sufficient yarn for this project.

The cable for this sweater is gorgeous but may seem intimidating. This is actually not as complex as it might appear, but I offer the following little hat which you can use either as a tension swatch or as a sample to see if you would like doing the cable pattern — or both. This has the additional advantage of checking your tension while knitting in the round. I don't recommend working tension swatches "flat" if the final product is to be knit in the round. Plus, I hate to do swatches, so here's a useful swatch.

CABLED HAT

Size: 17 (19)"/43 (48) cm

STARTING FROM THE TOP (WITH I-CORD)

Using 2 double-point needles, **Cast On** 3 stitches and work I-cord (see page 102) for approximately 1"/2.5 cm.

WHEEL OF HAT

The wheel has 6 sections. You will be increasing 6 stitches every second round. Change to the 4.0mm/US6 circular needle when you can.

Increase for wheel of hat:

Note: Use the increase of your choice. I used the Backward Loop which you can find on page 16.

Increase Round: *K1, Inc 1; repeat from * to end of round. (6 sts on needles)

Distribute stitches onto your set of double-point needles and work in the round.

Next Round: Knit.

Increase Round: *K1, Inc 1; repeat from * to end of round. (12 sts)

Next Round: Knit.

Increase Round: *K2, Inc 1; repeat from * to end of round. (18 sts)

Next Round: Knit.

Increase Round: *K3, Inc 1; repeat from * to end of round. (24 sts)

Next Round: Knit.

Increase Round: *Knit 4, Inc 1; repeat from * to end of round.

Next Round: Knit.

Continue increasing at the end of each of the 6 sections every 2nd round, until you have a total of 96 (108) sts. (16, 18 sts in each section).

RIDGE

Knit 1 round.

Purl 2 rounds.

Knit 1 round.

BODY OF HAT WITH CABLE PATTERN

There are three repeats of the cable panel around the hat with 10 (14) knit stitches in between each cable panel.

Increase Round: K5 (7), *work [K3, Inc 1] 6 times, K14 (18); repeat from * once more, work [K3, Inc 1] 6 times, K9 (11). (increasing 18 stitches - 114, 126 sts.)

Next Round: K5 (7), *P4, [K4, P4] 3 times, K10 (14); repeat from * twice more, ending the last repeat with K5 (7).

Second Size ONLY: Repeat the last round once more.

All Sizes:

To work the CABLE PANELS you have the choice of using written instructions or the Chart (see next page).

Next Round: K5 (7), *work CABLE PANEL, K10 (14); repeat from *, ending the last repeat with K5 (7).

Repeat the last round working through the 16 rounds of the Cable Panel.

Second Size ONLY:

Repeat the last round twice more, working Rounds 1 & 2 of the Cable Panel.

BOTTOM EDGE

Knit 1 round.

Decrease Round: K5 (7), *work [K2, K2tog] 6 times, K14 (18); repeat from * once more, work [K2, K2tog] 6 times, K9 (11). (96, 108 sts)

CABLE PANEL: You have the choice of using the written CABLE PANEL instructions (left column) or the CABLE PANEL CHART (below).

CABLE PANEL

Round 1: [P4, C4B] three times, P4.
Round 2: [P4, K4] three times, P4.
Round 3: P3, T3B, [T4F, T4B] twice, T3F, P3.
Round 4: P3, K2, P3, K4, P4, K4, P3, K2, P3.
Round 5: P2, T3B, P3, C4F, P4, C4F, P3, T3F, P2.
Round 6: P2, K2, P4, [K4, P4] twice, K2, P2.
Round 7: P2, K2, P3, T3B, T4F, T4B, T3F, P3, K2, P2.
Round 8: P2, [K2, P3] twice, K4, [P3, K2] twice, P2.
Round 9: P2, [K2, P3] twice, C4B, [P3, K2] twice, P2.
Round 10: Work Round 8.
Round 11: P2, K2, P3, T3F, T4B, T4F, T3B, P3, K2, P2.
Round 12: Work Round 6.
Round 13: P2, T3F, P3, C4F, P4, C4F, P3, T3B, P2.
Round 14: Work Round 4.
Round 15: P3, T3F, [T4B, T4F] twice, T3B, P3.
Round 16: Work Round 2.
Repeat these 16 rounds.

C4B (Cable 4 Back) slip next 2 sts onto cable needle and hold at back of work, knit next 2 sts from left-hand needle, then knit sts from cable needle.

C4F (Cable 4 Front) slip next 2 sts onto cable needle and hold at front of work, knit next 2 sts from left-hand needle, then knit sts from cable needle.

T3B (Twist 3 Back) slip next st onto cable needle and hold at back of work, knit next 2 sts from left-hand needle, then purl st from cable needle.

T3F (Twist 3 Front) slip next 2 sts onto cable needle and hold at front of work, purl next st from left-hand needle, then knit sts from cable needle.

T4B (Twist 4 Back) slip next 2 sts onto cable needle and hold at back of work, knit next 2 sts from left-hand needle, then purl sts from cable needle.

T4F (Twist 4 Front) slip next 2 sts onto cable needle and hold at front of work, purl next 2 sts from left-hand needle, then knit sts from cable needle.

CABLE PANEL CHART

knit
purl

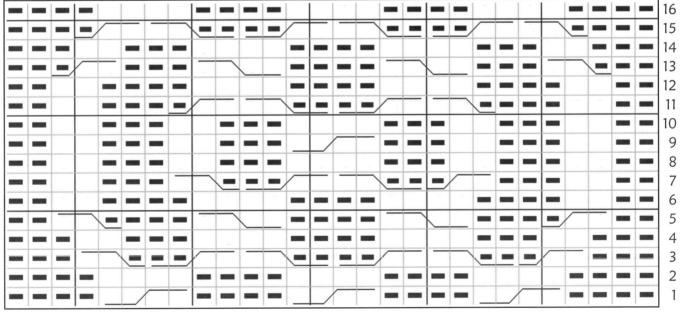

Purl 2 rounds for ridge.

Knit 1 round, decreasing 4 stitches evenly around for the second size only. (96, 104 sts)

Work [K2, P2] rib for 1 (1¼)"/2.5 (3) cm.

Cast off in [K2, P2] rib pattern. You may want to use a 4.5mm/US7 needle to cast off for a looser edge. Sew in ends.

CLASSIC CABLE SWEATER

Cast on with larger needle to ensure the sweater will go over your small person's head easily. Even when using the larger needle, do take care not to cast on too tightly.

TO BEGIN

With 4.5mm/US.7 needle **Cast On** 72 (80, 88, 96) stitches.

Next Round: With Body sized smaller circular needle, knit the stitches off the larger needle.

Join in the round being careful not to twist your stitches. Place a marker to indicate the beginning of the round.

Knit every round for ¾"/2 cm.

Next Round: Work [K2, P2] rib to end of round.

Repeat last round for 1"/2.5 cm.

Knit 1 round.

Purl 2 rounds.

Knit 1 round.

YOKE

Four shapelines are used to shape the yoke. Each shapeline consists of 2 stitches with a marker set in the centre of these 2 stitches. Every other round, increases are worked before and after each of the shapelines.

You will also place markers for the CABLE PANEL.

Marker Notes: Use four markers of the same colour to mark the CABLE PANELS. Use another 4 markers of another colour for the 4 shapelines.

The Beginning of Round Marker is also a shapeline marker but make it different in some way (I tie a piece of coloured yarn to the shapeline marker) so that you will know where each round begins.

Sounds confusing but once you get going you'll find the differently coloured markers always let you know where you are.

In the following round, place 4 Shapeline Markers and 4 Cable Panel Markers. Increases are worked inside the Cable Panel.

Marker Round: Slip Marker (this is Shapeline Marker#1), K3 (4, 5, 6), place Cable Panel Marker, [K4, Inc 1, K2, Inc 1] 3 times, K4, place Cable Panel Marker, K3 (4, 5, 6), place Shapeline Marker#2, K8 (10, 12, 14) sleeve stitches, place Shapeline Marker#3, K3 (4, 5, 6), place Cable Panel Marker, [K4, Inc 1, K2, Inc 1] 3 times, K4, place Cable Panel Marker, K3 (4, 5, 6), place Shapeline Marker#4, K8 (10, 12, 14) sleeve stitches. (84, 92, 100, 108 sts)

Reality check: You should have eight markers placed. Beginning of Round Marker#1 which also acts as a shapeline marker, Shapeline Markers#2, 3 & 4 in the same colour and four Cable Panel Markers in a second colour set before and after the two Cable Panels.

Note: Shapeline increases are indicated by "Inc 1". Use the increase method of your choice.

Set-Up Increase Round: Slip Marker#1, K1 (shapeline stitch), Inc 1, K2 (3, 4, 5), slip Cable Marker, P4, [K4, P4] 3 times, slip Cable Marker, K2 (3, 4, 5), Inc 1, K1 (shapeline stitch), slip Marker#2, K1 (shapeline stitch), Inc 1, K6 (8, 10, 12) for sleeve; Inc 1, K1 (shapeline stitch), slip Marker#3, K1 (shapeline stitch), Inc 1, K2 (3, 4, 5), slip Cable Marker, P4, [K4, P4] 3 times, slip Cable Marker, K2 (3, 4, 5), Inc 1, K1 (shapeline stitch), slip Marker#4, K1 (shapeline stitch), Inc 1, K6 (8, 10, 12) for sleeve, Inc 1, K1 (shapeline stitch). (92, 100, 108, 116 sts)

Straight Round: Slip first marker, knit to Cable Panel Marker, P4, [K4, P4] 3 times, slip Cable Marker, knit to next Cable Marker, P4, [K4, P4] 3 times, slip Cable Marker, knit to end of round.

Increase Round: *Slip Marker, K1, Inc 1, knit to Cable Marker, P4, [K4, P4] 3 times, slip Cable Marker, knit to 1 st before next shapeline marker, Inc 1, K1, slip marker (sm), K1, Inc 1, knit across sleeve to 1 st before next shapeline marker, Inc 1, K1; repeat from * once more. (100, 108, 116, 124 sts)

Work the CABLE using the chart or the written instructions as follows:

Straight Round: Slip Marker#1, knit to Cable Panel Marker, sm, work Round 1 of Cable Panel, slip Cable Panel marker, knit around to next Cable Panel Marker, sm, work Round 1 of Cable Panel, slip Cable Panel Marker, knit to end of round.

Increase Round: *Sm, K1 (shapeline), Inc 1, knit to cable marker, sm, work next round of Cable Panel, sm, knit to 1 st before next shapeline marker, Inc 1, K1, slip shapeline marker, K1, Inc 1, knit across sleeve to 1 stitch before next shapeline marker, Inc 1, K1; repeat from * once more.

Straight Round: Sm, knit to cable marker, sm, work next round of Cable Panel, sm, knit to next cable panel marker, sm, work next round of Cable Panel, sm, knit to end of round.

Repeat the last 2 rounds increasing as set and working through all 16 rounds of the Cable Panel then repeat the Cable Panel rounds until you have 220 (244, 260, 276) sts on your needle.

Reality Check: There should be 68 (74, 78, 82) stitches between the Markers for both the Body sections (includes the shapeline stitches). The sleeves should have 42 (48, 52, 56) stitches between the Markers. If you don't have this exact number don't worry about it, but try to fudge the numbers so that both the Body sections have the same number of stitches between the Markers, and both the sleeves have the same number.

Repeat Straight Round ONLY for an additional 1"/2.5 cm.

Divide Body and Sleeves: The Divide Round below will separate the sleeves and the body. The sleeve stitches will now be held on spare yarn as you work the Body first.

The Body stitches stay on the circular needle and stitches are cast on at the underarms.

At each shapeline, one shapeline stitch will go with the sleeve and one shapeline stitch with the Body stitches.

Divide Round: Sm, (remove the 3 shapeline markers as you go), *Knit to cable marker, work Cable Panel, knit to shapeline marker (68, 74, 78, 82 Body stitches which stay on the circular needle); K42 (48, 52, 56), thread the 42 (48, 52, 56) stitches just knit onto a spare piece of yarn for the sleeve; repeat from * once more. (136, 148, 156, 164 sts on circular needle for the Body.)

BODY

Set-Up Round: Sm, knit to cable marker, work Cable Panel, knit around to underarm, cast on 4 (4, 5, 7) stitches, knit to cable marker, work Cable Panel, knit around to underarm, cast on 4 (4, 5, 7) stitches. (144, 156, 166, 178 sts)

Next Round: Knit to cable marker, work Cable Panel, knit around to next cable marker, work Cable Panel, knit to end of round.

Repeat last round, until the sweater measures approximately 10 (11, 13, 15)"/25.5 (28, 33, 38) cm from the base of collar down to needle or 2"/5 cm shy of desired length for the child you are making it for, ending with a Round 3, 7, 11 or 15 of Cable Panel.

Next Round: Knit.

Decrease Round: Sm, *knit to cable marker, sm, K3, [K2tog, K2] 6 times, K1; repeat from * once more, knit to end of round. (132, 144, 154, 166 sts)

Purl 2 rounds.

Decrease Round: Knit, decreasing 12 (12, 10, 10) stitches evenly around sweater. (120, 132, 144, 156 sts)

Next Round: Work [K2, P2] rib to end of round.

Repeat last round for 1"/2.5 cm.

Knit every round for ¾"/2 cm.

Cast Off loosely.

SLEEVES

Set-Up Round: With dp needles and RS facing, starting in the centre of the underarm sts, pick up and knit 2 (2, 3, 4) stitches from the cast on edge of underarm sts, pick up an extra stitch here at the corner to help close the gap, knit the sleeve stitches on spare yarn, pick up an extra stitch here at the corner to help close the gap, pick up and knit 2 (2, 2, 3) sts to centre of underarm, place marker. (48, 54, 59, 65 sts)

Note: I don't think it is necessary to taper the sleeves for small children so I have put in directions for a straight sleeve for the 2 smallest sizes but you can taper the sleeves for all the sizes.

Straight Sleeve (2 smaller sizes): Knit every round until sleeve measures 4½ (6)"/11.5 (15) cm or to 2"/5 cm shy of desired length for the recipient of the sweater. Now work the Cuff.

- OR -

Taper the Sleeves:

Set-Up Round: Sizes 1 & 2 ONLY: Inc 1 st, knit to end of round. (49, 55 sts) The increased stitch becomes the underarm seamline stitch.

Begin Taper: (for all sizes)

Knit 7 rounds.

Next and every 8th round: K1, SSK, knit to 2 stitches before the end of the round, K2tog.

Repeat the last 8 rounds (Do not decrease to less than 41, 41, 45, 45 stitches), until sleeve measures 4½ (6, 8, 10)"/11.5 (15, 20.5, 25.5) cm or to 2"/5 cm shy of desired length for the recipient of the sweater. Now work the Cuff.

CUFF

Next Round (Straight Sleeve — Sizes 1 & 2 ONLY: K2tog, *K4 (2), K2tog; repeat from * 6 (12) times more, ending with K4 (0). (40 sts)

- OR -

Next Round (Tapered Sleeve): Knit, decreasing to 40 (40, 44, 44) sts.

Both Sleeves:

Purl 2 rounds.

Knit 1 round.

Next Round: Work [K2, P2] rib to end of round.

Repeat last round for 1"/2.5 cm.

Knit every round for ¾"/2 cm.

Cast Off. Sew in ends so that they can not be seen when the edges roll.

SWEATSHIRT STYLE

Experience Level: With Gusto!
(Enthusiastic Beginner)

adapted by Shirl the Purl

*The cropped sleeves stay dry when
playing in mud or water and the pouch
is perfect for warming up little hands.*

ABBREVIATIONS:

(RS): Right side (public side) of work.

(WS): Wrong side of work.

M1: Make one stitch (no holes). With the left needle lift the running thread between the stitch just worked and the next stitch, from front to back, and knit into the back of the resulting loop.

pm: Place a marker.

sm: Slip the marker.

K2tog: Right slanting decrease: Knit the next two stitches together.

st(s): Stitch(es).

SSK: Left leaning decrease: Slip the next stitch as if to knit, slip the next stitch as if to knit, insert the left needle into the fronts of the two slipped stitches on the right needle. Knit the 2 slipped stitches together.

Your munchkin will be warm and comfortable in this casual unisex pullover.

Needles:

4.0mm/US6 circular needle (16"/40 cm long)

4.0mm/US6 circular needle (24"/60 cm long)

4.0mm/US6 double-point needles (for "no sew" sleeves)

Tension:

22 stitches = 4"/10 cm on 4.0mm/US6 needle in stocking stitch or needle needed to obtain this tension.

Directions are given for size 1, other sizes are in brackets. If only one figure is shown, it applies to all sizes.

To Fit:	1 year	2 year	4 year	6 year
Chest Size of:	20" 51 cm	22" 56 cm	24" 61 cm	26" 66 cm
Finished Size:				
Chest	24" 61 cm	26" 66 cm	28" 71 cm	30" 76 cm
Sleeve Length from underarm	4½" 11.5 cm	5½" 14 cm	7½" 19 cm	9½" 24 cm
Body Length	12" 30.5 cm	13" 33 cm	15" 38 cm	17" 43 cm

Materials: DK Yarn - 50g ball, 112m/123yds

Main Colour	4	4	5	6
Ring markers	4	4	4	4

The Sweatshirt Style shown was knit with Patons BumbleBee Baby Cotton in colour #2714.

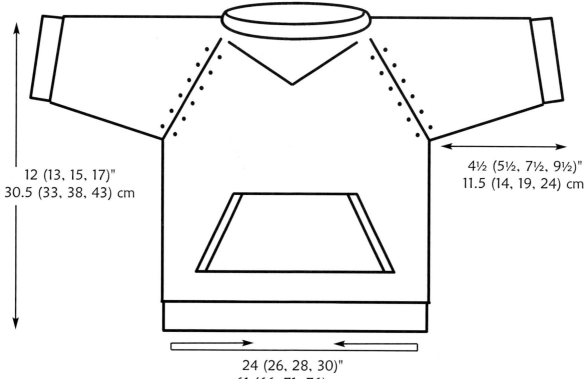

12 (13, 15, 17)"
30.5 (33, 38, 43) cm

4½ (5½, 7½, 9½)"
11.5 (14, 19, 24) cm

24 (26, 28, 30)"
61 (66, 71, 76) cm

Sweatshirt Style

TO BEGIN

With shorter circular needle **Cast On** 72 (80, 88, 96) stitches loosely. Join in the round, being careful not to twist the stitches. Place a marker to indicate beginning of a round. The round begins at the centre back of the neck.

NECKBAND

Rib Round: Work in [K2, P2] rib to end of round.

Repeat last round 4 more times.

YOKE

All rounds begin at the centre Back.

Marker Round: P14 (15, 16, 17) for the Right Back, place a marker; P8 (10, 12, 14) for Right Sleeve, place a marker; P28 (30, 32, 34) for Front, place a marker; P8 (10, 12, 14) for Left Sleeve, place a marker; purl to end of round for Left Back.

Begin Increases:

The sample uses a M1 increase.

Increase Round 1: Knit to 1 stitch before the next marker, M1, K1, slip marker; K1, M1, knit to 1 stitch before marker, M1, K1, sm; K1, M1, purl to 1 stitch before marker, M1, K1, sm; K1, M1, knit to 1 stitch before marker, M1, K1, sm; K1, M1, knit to end of round.

Eight stitches have been increased and the Front Neck **V** motif begun.

Round 2: [Knit to marker, sm] twice; K3, purl until 3 stitches remain before the next marker, K3, sm; knit to the next marker, sm; knit to the end of the round.

Increase Round 3: Knit to 1 stitch before the next marker, M1, K1, sm; K1, M1, knit to 1 stitch before the marker, M1, K1, sm; K1, M1, K3, purl to 4 stitches before the marker, K3, M1, K1, sm; K1, M1, knit to 1 stitch before marker, M1, K1, sm; K1, M1, knit to end of the round.

Round 4: [Knit to marker, sm] twice, K6, purl until 6 stitches remain before the marker, K6, sm; knit to the marker, sm; knit to end of the round.

Rounds 3 & 4 establish the increase pattern and the purled **V** at the Front Neck.

Repeat Rounds 3 & 4, increasing at each shapeline on the odd numbered rounds and on the Front, working 1 more knit stitch at each side of the **V** every round, until all **V** stitches are worked as knits. The **V** motif will be complete.

Change to the longer circular needle when work becomes tight.

Continue increasing on odd numbered rounds and knitting even rounds until you have the following number of stitches:

1 year: 31 Right Back, 42 Right Sleeve, 62 Front, 42 Left Sleeve, 31 Left Back. (208 sts)

2 years: 34 RB, 48 RS, 68 F, 48 LS, 34 LB. (232 sts)

4 years: 36 RB, 52 RS, 72 F, 52 LS, 36 LB. (248 sts)

6 years: 38 RB, 56 RS, 76 F, 56 LS, 38 LB. (264 sts)

Knit every round, without increasing, until work measures 7 (8, 8½, 9)"/18 (20.5, 21.5, 23) cm from the cast on edge when measured at the Centre Front.

NOTE: If, through inattention or misadventure, you have missed an increase or two, you can add increases on these plain rounds.

DIVIDE FOR BODY AND SLEEVES

Next Round: Knit to the first marker, remove marker, [place next 42 (48, 52, 56) Sleeve stitches on a holder, remove marker; cast on 4 (4, 5, 7) stitches for underarm]; knit to the next marker for Front, remove marker; repeat [ ] once; knit to the end of the round leaving beginning marker in place. (132, 144, 154, 166 sts on needle for Body)

All Sizes:

Knit every round for 1"/2.5 cm.

POUCH

Set-Up Round: K50 (54, 58, 62); [K1, P1] twice, P24 (28, 30, 34), [P1, K1] twice; knit to end of the round.

Next Row: K50 (54, 58, 62); leave stitches just worked on the longer circular needle; using the shorter circular needle [K1, P1] twice, M1, K24 (28, 30, 34), M1, [P1, K1] twice.

Note: You now have 34 (38, 40, 44) sts on short circular needle for the pouch.

Leaving the body stitches on the longer circular needle, work back and forth on the pouch stitches with the shorter circular as follows:

Next Row: Turn work and with Wrong Side of pouch stitches facing, [P1, K1] twice, P26 (30, 32, 36), [K1, P1] twice, turn. (34, 38, 40, 44 sts)

Row 1: (RS) [K1, P1] twice, knit to the last 4 stitches, [P1,K1] twice.

Row 2: (WS) [P1, K1] twice, purl to the last 4 stitches, [K1, P1] twice.

Row 3 (increase row): [K1, P1] twice, M1, knit to last 5 stitches, M1, [P1, K1] twice.

Row 4: as Row 2.

Repeat last 4 rows 5 (6, 8, 9) more times. (46, 52, 58, 64 pouch stitches)

Break yarn. Leave pouch stitches on the shorter circular needle.

BODY

Resume working with the stitches on the longer circular needle as follows:

With Right Side facing, rejoin yarn at the first body stitch after the pouch, knit to the end of the round at centre Back.

Note: In the next round you need to pick up stitches from underneath the Pouch to continue with the Body. Pick up and knit the stitches from the round below the groove created by the purl stitches on the Front.

Set-up Round: Knit to Pouch opening, lifting the Pouch and working on the underside, pick up and knit 1 stitch in the back of each of the 4 ribbed stitches that mark the beginning of the Pouch; pick up and knit 1 stitch in the purl bump of each Pouch stitch in the row below the groove; pick up and knit 1 stitch in the back of each of the 4 ribbed stitches that mark the left edge of the Pouch (32, 36, 38, 42 Pouch stitches picked up); knit to end of round.

Note: Because you are picking up the top edge of a previously worked stitch and knitting downwards from it, finding the right number of Pouch stitches can be tricky. If you are short a few stitches simply increase to the correct number (evenly spaced) when you come to the Pouch in the next round. These increases will be hidden when the Pouch is complete.

Knit every round for 24 (28, 36, 40) rounds. Pouch and body should now be the same length.

Unite Pouch and Body: K43 (46, 48, 51) stitches, knit the pouch stitches together with the body stitches by working K2tog (one pouch stitch and one body stitch) 46 (52, 58, 64) times in all across pouch; knit to end of round. (132, 144, 154, 166 sts.)

Knit 6 rounds.

Next Round: Purl, decreasing 0 (0, 2 ,2) stitches evenly spaced.

BOTTOM RIB

Work in [K2, P2] rib for 10 rounds.

Cast off loosely, in ribbing.

CROPPED SLEEVES

Transfer sleeve stitches from holder to double-pointed needles, dividing them evenly.

Next Round: Beginning at the centre of the underarm, with the remaining dpn, pick up and knit 2 (2, 3, 4) stitches from the cast on edge of the underarm stitches, pick up 1 stitch in the corner, knit across the sleeve stitches, pick up 1 stitch in the corner, pick up and knit 2 (2, 2, 3) stitches to the centre of the underarm, place marker. (48, 54, 59, 65 sts)

NOTE: Keep count of the total number of Sleeve rounds worked so that both will be identical.

Size 1 & 2 years ONLY:

Knit every round, without decreasing, until sleeve measures 3 (4)"/7.5 (10) cm from underarm, or until work measures 1½"/4 cm from desired length.

Next Round: Purl, decreasing 8 (10) stitches evenly spaced. 40 (44) sts.

Now work the Cuff.

Size 4 & 6 years ONLY:

Rounds 1-7: Knit.

Round 8 (Decrease Round): K1, K2tog, knit until 2 stitches remain before marker, SSK.

Repeat these 8 rounds until the sleeve measures 6 (8)"/15 (20.5) cm from underarm, or until work measures 1½"/4 cm from the desired length.

Next Round: Purl, decreasing to 44 stitches.

CUFF

Work in [K2, P2] ribbing for 10 rounds.

Cast off loosely in ribbing.

"No-sew knitting gives you a psychological advantage! There is no worrying suspense about how it will all come together in the end."

WOVEN RIDGES

Experience Level: Intermediate

designed by Deb Gemmell

ABBREVIATIONS:

Inc 1: Increase 1 stitch. See Increases on page 16 for descriptions of various increase methods.

K2tog: Right slanting decrease. Knit the next two stitches together.

M1 (Make one): Make one stitch (no holes). With the left needle lift the running thread between the stitch just worked and the next stitch, from front to back, and knit into the back of the resulting loop.

pm: Place a marker.

sm: Slip the marker.

SSK: Left leaning decrease. Slip the next stitch as if to knit, slip the next stitch as if to knit, insert the left needle into the fronts of the two slipped stitches on the right needle. Knit the 2 slipped stitches together.

This understated classic with a stylish twist really lets your knitting skill shine through. Why not knit it up in your favourite team colour?

Needles:

5.0mm/US8 needle - Collar Cast On ONLY
4.0mm/US6 circular needle (40cm/16" long)
Optional for two larger sizes:
4.0mm/US6 circular needle (60cm/24" long)
1 set of 4.0mm/US6 double-point needles for the sleeves.

Tension:

22 stitches = 4"/10 cm on 4.0mm/US6 needle in stocking stitch or needle needed to obtain this tension.

Directions are given for size 1, other sizes are in brackets. If only one figure is shown, it applies to all sizes.

To Fit:	1 year	2 year	4 year	6 year
Chest Size of:	20"	22"	24"	26"
	51 cm	56 cm	61 cm	66 cm
Finished Size:				
Chest	24"	26"	28"	30"
	61 cm	66 cm	71 cm	76 cm
Sleeve Length	6½"	8"	10"	12"
	16.5 cm	20.5 cm	25.5 cm	30.5 cm
Body Length	12"	13"	15"	17"
	30.5 cm	33 cm	38 cm	43 cm

Materials: DK Yarn - 50g ball, 119m/130yds

	1 year	2 year	4 year	6 year
Main Colour	4	5	6	7
Ring markers	8	8	8	8

The Woven Ridges left was worked in Butterfly Super 10 cotton in Periwinkle #3882; the Woven Ridges below was knit in Shelridge Farm's Soft Touch W4 in Cranberry.

BEGIN WITH RIB COLLAR

Cast on with larger needle to ensure the sweater will go over the head easily.

TO BEGIN

With 5.0mm/US8 **Cast On** 80 (80, 96, 96) stitches.

Next Round: With smaller circular needle, work the stitches off the larger needle as follows: K1, P2, *K2, P2; repeat from * to last stitch, K1.

Join in the round being careful not to twist your stitches. Place a marker to indicate the beginning of the round.

Repeat last round and rib for 1½ (2, 2, 2)"/4 (5, 5, 5) cm.

YOKE

Four shapelines are used to shape the yoke. Each shapeline consists of 2 stitches. Every other round, increases are worked before and after each shapeline. In the next round you will place a marker in the centre of each of the 4 shapelines.

Note: Make the First Marker different in some way (a different colour or tie a piece of coloured yarn to it) so that you will know where each round begins.

SET-UP WOVEN RIDGE PATTERN

Ridge Round 1: *Slip marker (sm), K1 (shapeline stitch), P6, [K2, P6] 3 (3, 4, 4) times for the Body; K1 (shapeline stitch), Place Marker, K1 (shapeline stitch), P6 for the sleeve; K1 (shapeline stitch), Place Marker, K1 (shapeline stitch), P6, [K2, P6] 3 (3, 4, 4) times for the Body; K1 (shapeline stitch), Place Marker, K1 (shapeline stitch), P6 for sleeve, K1 (shapeline stitch).

Ridge Round 2: *Sm, K1, P6, [K2, P6] 3 (3, 4, 4) times, K1, sm, K1, P6, K1; repeat from * once more.

Increase Round 3: *Sm, K1 (shapeline), M1, P2, [K2, P2] 7 (7, 9, 9) times, M1, K1, sm, K1, M1, K6, M1, K1; repeat from * once more.

Straight Round 4: *Sm, [K2, P2] 8 (8, 10, 10) times, K2, sm, K10; repeat from * once more.

Increase Round 5: *Sm, K1, M1, K1, P2, [K2, P2] 7 (7, 9, 9) times, K1, M1, K1, sm, K1, M1, K8, M1, K1; repeat from * once more.

In next round place markers for centre Rib Panel.

Straight Round 6: *Sm, K3, place panel marker, P2, [K2, P2] 7 (7, 9, 9) times, place panel marker, K3, sm, K12; repeat from * once more.

Increase Round 7: *Sm, K1, M1, knit to panel marker, P2, [K2, P2] 7 (7, 9, 9) times across panel, knit to 1 stitch before shapeline marker, M1, K1, sm, K1, M1, knit across sleeve to 1 stitch before next shapeline marker, M1, K1; repeat from * once more.

Straight Round 8: *Sm, knit to centre panel, work panel as set, knit around to next centre panel marker, work panel as set, knit to end of round.

Continue with WOVEN RIDGE PATTERN, see box, *starting at Ridge (increase) Round 9.*

Repeat the 16 rounds of the WOVEN RIDGE PATTERN until you have 208 (224, 240, 256) stitches on your needle.

Reality Check: There should be 64 (68, 76, 80) stitches between the shapeline Markers for both the Body sections. The sleeves should have 40 (44, 44, 48) stitches between the Markers. If you don't have this exact number don't worry about it, but try to fudge the numbers so that both the Body sections have the same number of stitches between the Markers and both the sleeves have the same number.

Measure the Yoke vertically down the centre Back from the top of the first ridge at the base of the collar down to your needle. If it is 6 (7, 7½, 8)"/15 (18, 19, 20.5) cm deep continue with Divide Body and Sleeves. If necessary, continue to work in Woven Ridge Pattern (BODY, page 78), without any more increases, until you have reached the length above.

Divide Body and Sleeves: The Divide Round below will separate the sleeves and the body. The sleeve stitches will now be held on spare yarn as you work the Body first.

YOKE - WOVEN RIDGE

Ridge (Increase) Round 1: *Sm, K1, M1, purl to centre panel, P6, [K2, P6] 3 (3, 4, 4) times, purl to 1 stitch before marker, M1, K1, sm, K1, M1, purl to 1 stitch before marker, M1, K1; repeat from * once more.

Ridge Round 2: *Sm, K1, purl to centre panel, P6, [K2, P6] 3 (3, 4, 4) times, purl to 1 stitch before marker, K1, sm, K1, purl to 1 stitch before next marker, K1; repeat from * once more.

Increase Round 3: *Sm, K1, M1, knit to centre panel, P2, [K2, P2] 7 (7, 9, 9) times, knit to 1 stitch before shapeline marker, M1, K1, sm, K1, M1, knit to 1 stitch before shapeline marker, M1, K1; repeat from * once more.

Straight Round 4: Sm, knit to centre panel, P2, [K2, P2] 7 (7, 9, 9) times, knit around to centre panel, P2, [K2, P2] 7 (7, 9, 9) times, knit to end of round.

Rounds 5-8: Repeat Rounds 3 and 4 two more times (total of 6 knit rounds).

Ridge (Increase) Round 9: *Sm, K1, M1, purl to panel marker, P2, [K2, P6] 3 (3, 4, 4) times, K2, P2, purl to 1 stitch before shapeline marker, M1, K1, sm, K1, M1, purl to 1 stitch before next shapeline marker, M1, K1; repeat from * once more.

Ridge Round 10: *Sm, K1, purl to centre panel, P2, [K2, P6] 3 (3, 4, 4) times, K2, P2, purl to 1 stitch before shapeline marker, K1, sm, K1, purl to 1 stitch before shapeline marker, K1; repeat from * once more.

Increase Round 11: *Sm, K1, M1, knit to centre panel, P2, [K2, P2] 7 (7, 9, 9) times, knit to 1 stitch before shapeline marker, M1, K1, sm, K1, M1, knit to 1 stitch before shapeline marker, M1, K1; repeat from * once more.

Straight Round 12: Sm, knit to centre panel, P2, [K2, P2] 7 (7, 9, 9) times, knit around to centre panel, P2, [K2, P2] 7 (7, 9, 9) times, knit to end of round.

Rounds 13-16: Repeat Rounds 11 & 12 two more times.

The Body stitches stay on the circular needle and stitches are cast on at the underarms.

At each shapeline, one stitch will go with the sleeve and one stitch with the Body stitches.

Divide Round: Remove markers as you go, *Work in pattern as set to centre panel, work panel as set, work to next shapeline marker (64, 68, 76, 80 stitches - these are the Body stitches); work in pattern as set across 40 (44, 44, 48) stitches of sleeve to next shapeline marker , thread these 40 (44, 44, 48) sleeve stitches onto a spare piece of yarn; repeat from * once more. (128, 136, 152, 160 sts on circular needle for the Body.)

BODY

Continue with the Woven Ridge Pattern (without increases) and place a marker in the centre of underarm in the next round.

Next Round: Work in pattern as set to underarm, Cast On 3 (5, 3, 5) stitches, work in pattern as set to underarm, Cast On 1 (2, 1, 2) stitches, Place Marker, Cast On 2 (3, 2, 3). (134, 146, 158, 170 sts)

Next Round: Finish the round in pattern, to underarm marker.

All Rounds now begin at the underarm marker.

Continue to work the Woven Ridge Pattern (BODY) without increases, ending after working a RIDGE, until the sweater measures approximately 10 (11, 13, 15)"/25.5 (28, 33, 38) cm from first ridge at base of collar down to needle or 2"/5 cm shy of desired length for the child you are making it for.

In the next round, stitches are decreased in the side knit panels on either side of the centre panels so that the ribbing for the bottom edge will line up with the centre panel rib as established.

Decrease Round: Knit across side panel to centre panel, decreasing 4 (5, 4, 5) stitches evenly in this side panel, work centre panel in pattern, knit across 2 side panels to next centre panel, decreasing evenly 7 (9, 7, 9) stitches, work centre panel in pattern, knit to end of round, decreasing evenly 3 (4, 3, 4) stitches in this last side panel. (120, 128, 144, 152 sts)

Next Round: K1, P2, work [K2, P2] rib around, ending with K1.

Note: Ribbing should line up correctly with the centre panels.

Work rib as set for 2"/5 cm or desired length.

Cast Off in rib pattern.

SLEEVES

Set-Up Round: With double-point needles and RS facing, starting in the centre of the underarm stitches, pick up and knit 2 (3, 3, 3) stitches from the cast on underarm stitches, pick up an extra stitch here to help close the gap, knit the sleeve stitches on spare yarn, pick up an extra stitch here to help close the gap, pick up and knit 1 (2, 2, 2) stitches to centre of underarm, place marker. (45, 51, 51, 55 sts)

Taper the Sleeve

Work in pattern as set until you are ready to work the next ridge.

Ridge (Decrease) Round 1: P1, P2tog, purl to 2 stitches before the end of the round, P2tog.

Ridge Round 2: Purl.

Knit 6 rounds.

Repeat last 8 rounds, decreasing on every first Ridge Round until there are 41 (41, 45, 45 sts).

SLEEVE - RIDGE PATTERN

Purl 2 rounds.

Knit 6 rounds.

Continue to work the sleeve straight in Ridge Pattern until it measures approximately 4½ (6, 8, 10)"/11.5 (15, 20.5, 25.5) cm (*ending after*

working a ridge) or 2"/5 cm shy of desired length for the recipient of the sweater.

Note: If the last ridge ends up to be short of the length above, just work the ribbing longer for the correct sleeve length.

Decrease Round: Knit around, decreasing to 40 (40, 44, 44) stitches.

Work in (K2, P2) rib for 2"/5 cm or to desired length.

Cast Off in rib pattern.

Sew in ends.

BODY - WOVEN RIDGE (NO INCREASES)

Ridge Round 1: Sm, *purl to centre panel, P6, [K2, P6] 3 (3, 4, 4) times; repeat from * once more, purl to end of round.

Ridge Round 2: Sm, *purl to centre panel, P6, [K2, P6] 3 (3, 4, 4) times; repeat from * once more, purl to end of round.

Round 3: Sm, *knit to centre panel, P2, [K2, P2] 7 (7, 9, 9) times; repeat from * once more, knit to end of round.

Rounds 4-8: Repeat last round, 5 more times (6 times in total).

Ridge Round 9: Sm, *purl to panel marker, P2, [K2, P6] 3 (3, 4, 4) times, K2, P2; repeat from * once more, purl to end of round.

Ridge Round 10: Sm, *Purl to centre panel, P2, [K2, P6] 3 (3, 4, 4) times, K2, P2; repeat from * once more, purl to end of round.

Round 11: Sm, *knit to centre panel, P2, [K2, P2] 7 (7, 9, 9) times; repeat from * once more, knit to end of round.

Rounds 12-16: Repeat last round, 5 more times (6 times in total).

FLORABEL

Experience Level: Intermediate

adapted by Maureen Mason-Jamieson

ABBREVIATIONS:

BB: Big centre bobble (see next page).

Inc 1: Increase 1 stitch. See Increases on page 16 for descriptions of various increase methods.

K2tog: Right slanting decrease: Knit the next two stitches together.

pm: Place a marker.

SB: Small bobble (see next page).

SSK: Left leaning decrease: Slip the next stitch as if to knit, slip the next stitch as if to knit, insert the left needle into the fronts of the two slipped stitches on the right needle. Knit the 2 slipped stitches together.

sm: Slip the marker.

yo: Yarn Over to make a hole (eyelet) and increase one stitch: Bring wool under the right needle and forward to the front of your work, swing the wool over the right needle to the back of your work and knit the next stitch. The resulting loop is worked as a stitch in the next row or round.

Feminine and fashionable, Florabel's matching pullover and hat make little girl look as fresh and colourful as a bouquet.

Needles:

5.0mm/US8 needle - Collar Cast On ONLY
4.0mm/US6 circular needle (40 cm/16" long)
Optional for two larger sizes:
4.0mm/US6 circular needle (60 cm/24" long)
1 set of 4.0mm/US6 double-point needles for the sleeves.

Tension:

22 stitches = 4"/10 cm on 4.0mm/US6 needle in stocking stitch or needle needed to obtain this tension.

Directions are given for size 1, other sizes are in brackets. If only one figure is shown, it applies to all sizes.

FLOWER BOBBLES:

Small Bobble (SB): Using CC1, (k1, yo, k1, yo, k1) in next stitch - 5 sts on needle. Turn. Beginning with a purl row, work 4 rows stockinette. With RS facing, pass second, third, fourth and fifth stitches over the first stitch on needle.

Big centre Bobble (BB): With left needle, pick up the horizontal bar between stitch just knit and the next stitch. Using CC2, (k1, yo, k1, yo, k1, yo, k1) into bar stitch - 7 sts on needle. Turn. Beginning with a purl row, work 6 rows stockinette. With RS facing, pass second, third, fourth, fifth, sixth and seventh stitches over the first stitch on needle. Big bobble lies centered in middle of 4 knit sts of previous round. Slip remaining CC1 bobble stitch to left needle, knit it together with next stitch.

To Fit:	1 year	2 year	4 year	6 year
Chest Size of:	20"	22"	24"	26"
	51 cm	56 cm	61 cm	66 cm
Finished Size:				
Chest	24"	26"	28"	30"
	61 cm	66 cm	71 cm	76 cm
Sleeve Length	6½"	8"	10"	12"
	16.5 cm	20.5 cm	25.5 cm	30.5 cm
Body Length	12"	13"	15"	17"
	30.5 cm	33 cm	38 cm	43 cm
Hat:	17½"	17½"	18"	19"
	44.5 cm	44.5 cm	45.5 cm	48 cm

Materials: DK Yarn - 50g ball, 119m/130yds

Pullover:				
Main Colour	4	5	6	7
Contrast Colour 1	1	1	1	1
Contrast Colour 2	½	½	½	½
Hat:				
Main Colour	1	1	1	1
Contrast Colour 1	1	1	1	1
Contrast Colour 2	½	½	½	½
Ring markers	4	4	4	4

Florabel options: You could knit your bobble flowers in a variegated or handpainted yarn on plain MC (or vice versa!). Knit bobble flowers from sparkly eyelash or fancy yarns to create a bouquet fit for a princess. If the thought of embroidery doesn't make you faint — 2 black dots and a "V" make a happy face in the middle of the centre big bobble.

"I like garments that capture the imagination in some way — that are just a little different."

TO BEGIN

Follow the Basic Top-Down Pullover from beginning to BODY section with (124, 136, 144, 152 sts on circular needle for the Body).

BODY

Next Round: Place a marker for the beginning of the round, knit to underarm, Cast On 4 (4, 5, 7) sts, knit to underarm, Cast On 4 (4, 5, 7) stitches.   (132, 144, 154, 166 sts)

Knit every round until the Body measures 7 (8, 10, 12)"/ 18 (20.5, 25.5, 30.5) cm from the base of the collar down to needle or 5"/ 13 cm shy of desired length for the child you are making it for.

Sizes 4 and 6 year ONLY:

In the following round increase 2 stitches to accommodate the Bobble Flower Pattern.

Next Round: K38 (41), Inc 1 stitch, K78 (84), Inc 1 stitch, knit to end of round.

ALL SIZES

Reality Check: The Front of the sweater now has 66 (72, 78, 84) stitches in order to accommodate the Bobble Flower Pattern and 132 (144, 156, 168) stitches in total on the circular needle.

FLOWER BOBBLES

To avoid long floats that may catch on little fingers work each Small Bobble with CC1 and break yarn after each bobble as you work across the front OR work the pair of bobbles in each repeat and then break the CC1 yarn and join back in for the next flower.

- OR -

To avoid sewing in lots of ends, cut 1 length of CC1 - 4 yds/3.65 m long for each of the 5 bobble flowers. Use this one length for all the small bobbles in the same flower as follows: For each flower work the two Small Bobble of each repeat with the length of CC1. In the second round pull the CC1 yarn back across the flower into position, careful not to pull it too tightly and pucker the flower, then work the next pair of small bobbles.

You will need 1yd. of CC2 for each centre big bobble.

DO NOT CARRY CONTRAST COLOURS ACROSS THE SWEATER BACK.

Place 5 bobble flowers across Front of body:
Bobble Flower Round 1: With MC, K5 (6, 7, 8), *[with CC1 work SB (small bobble), with MC K2, with CC1 work SB, with MC K9 (10, 11, 12) stitches to next flower]; repeat from * 3 more times, work last flower [with CC1 SB, with MC K2, with CC1 SB], with MC knit to end of round. -- you have 5 flowers with 2 CC1 bobbles in each flower across sweater Front.

Round 2: With MC, K4 (5, 6, 7), *[with CC1 SB, with MC K4, with CC1 SB, with MC K7 (8, 9, 10) stitches]; repeat from * 3 more times, work last flower [with CC1 SB, with MC K4, with CC1 SB], with MC knit to end of round.

Round 3: With MC, K7 (8, 9, 10) stitches, *[with CC2 BB (big bobble) using horizontal bar in between stitches, with MC K13 (14, 15, 16) stitches]; repeat from * 3 more times, work last flower [with CC2 BB], with MC knit to end of round.

Round 4: As Round 2.

Round 5: As Round 1.

Bobble Flowers completed.

Knit every round until the sweater measures 10 (11, 13, 15)"/25.5 (28, 33, 38) cm from the base of collar down to needle or 2"/5 cm shy of desired length for the child you are making it for.

Next Round: Knit around, decreasing 10 stitches evenly around the Body.

Knit every round for 2½"/6.5 cm. (The extra ½"/1.5 cm is for the rolled edge). **Cast off.**

SLEEVES

Follow Tapered Sleeve option of The Basic Pullover Pattern. Decrease to 41 (41, 45, 45) stitches as directed.

Knit every round until sleeve measures 4 (5½, 7½, 9½)"/ 10 (14, 19, 24) cm or to 2½"/ 6.5 cm shy of desired length for the recipient of the sweater.

Next Round: Knit, decreasing 1 stitch. (40, 40, 44, 44 sts)

FLOWER BOBBLES:

Work with CC1 as you did for the Body flowers. Do Not carry contrast colours from flower to flower. It is important to avoid any floats where little fingers can get caught.

Place 3 bobble flowers across sleeve:

Sleeve Bobble Flower Round 1: With MC, K6 (6, 8, 8), *[with CC1 SB (small bobble) , with MC K2, with CC1 SB, with MC K8], repeat from * once more, work last flower [with CC1 SB, with MC K2, with CC1 SB], with MC knit to end of round. (6 CC1 bobbles knit in across sleeve)

Round 2: With MC, K5 (5, 7, 7), *[with CC1 SB, with MC K4, with CC1 SB, with MC K6], repeat from * once more, work last flower [with CC1 SB, with MC K4, with CC1 SB], with MC knit to end of round.

Round 3: With MC, K8 (8, 10, 10), * [with CC2 BB (big bobble), with MC K12], repeat from * once more, work last flower [with CC2 BB], with MC knit to end of round.

Round 4: As Round 2.

Round 5: As Round 1.

Knit every round until sleeve measures 7 (8½, 10½, 12½)"/18 (21.5, 26.5, 32) cm or desired length to complete sleeve. (The extra ½"/1.5 cm is for the rolled edge.) **Cast off.**

Sew in ends so that they can not be seen when the edges roll. Block and enjoy!

FLORABEL HAT

I have only included 3 sizes for the hat. If possible, have the circumference of the child's head measured as head size can greatly vary between child to child.

STARTING FROM THE TOP (with I-cord)

With Contrast Colour 2 (CC2) and 2 double-point needles, Cast On 4 stitches and work I-cord for approximately 5"/13 cm (see page 102). Cut CC2 leaving 4"/10 cm tail (which will be used to tack the tail into a knot).

WHEEL OF HAT

The wheel has 8 sections. You will be increasing 8 stitches every second round. Change to the circular needle when you can unless you prefer dp needles.

INCREASE FOR WHEEL OF HAT:

Increase Round: With Main Colour, *K1, Inc 1 (using increase of your choice) repeat from * to end of round. (8 sts on needles)

Distribute stitches onto your set of double-point needles and work in the round.

Note: You may find it easier to distribute onto 2 double-point needles and knit with a third needle at this point and then distribute onto your full set of double-point needles after the next set of increases.

Next Round: Knit 1 round.

Increase Round: *K1, Inc 1; repeat from * to end of round. (16 sts)

Bobble Round: *With MC K1, with CC1 work Small Bobble (SB); repeat from * to end of round. Cut CC1. (8 bobbles)

Continue with Main Colour for crown of hat:

Increase Round: *K2, Inc 1; repeat from * to end of round. (24 sts)

Next Round: Knit 1 round.

Increase Round: *K3, Inc 1; repeat from * to end of round. (32 sts)

Next Round: Knit 1 round.

Increase Round: *Knit 4, Inc 1; repeat from * to end of round.

Next Round: Knit 1 round.

Continue increasing at the end of each of the 8 sections every 2nd round, until you have a total of 96 (96, 104) sts. (12, 12, 13 sts in each of the 8 sections).

BODY OF HAT

Knit 1 round increasing 0 (4, 0) stitches evenly across round. (96, 100, 104 sts)

Purl 3 rounds for ridge.

Knit every round for body of hat until it measures 1 (1, 1½)"/2.5 (2.5, 4) cm from ridge.

FLOWER BOBBLES

CC1 may be carried between bobble flowers if desired. Or to avoid long floats that may catch on little fingers work each Small Bobble with CC1 and break yarn after each bobble as you work around OR work the pair of bobbles in each repeat and then break the yarn, join yarn back in for the next flower.

You will need 1 yard of CC2 for each centre big bobble.

SIZES 17½ AND 19" ONLY

Round 1: With MC, K4, *[with CC1 work SB (small bobble), with MC K2, with CC1 work SB, with MC K8 (9)]; repeat from * 6 more times, work last flower [with CC1 work SB, with MC K2, with CC1 work SB, with MC K4 (5)]. (you have 16 CC1 bobbles around hat.)

Round 2: With MC, K3, *[with CC1 work SB, with MC K4, with CC1 work SB, with MC K6 (7) stitches]; repeat from * 6 more times, work last flower [with CC1 work SB, with MC K4, with CC1 work SB, with MC 3 (4) stitches]. Cut CC1.

Round 3: With MC, K6, * [with CC2 work BB (big bobble) using horizontal bar in between stitches, with MC K12, (13) stitches]; repeat from * 6 more times, work last flower [with CC2 work BB using horizontal bar in between stitches, with MC K6 (7) stitches]. Cut CC2.

Round 4: As Round 2.

Round 5: As Round 1.

SIZE: 18" ONLY

Round 1: With MC, K4 stitches, *[with CC1 SB, with MC K2, with CC1 SB, with MC K8, with CC1 SB, with MC K2, with CC1 SB, with MC K9]; repeat from * 2 more times, end [with CC1 SB, with MC K2, with CC1 SB, with MC K8, with CC1 SB, with MC K2, with CC1 SB, with MC K5] (You have 16 CC1 bobbles knit in around hat.)

Round 2: With MC, K3 stitches, *[with CC1 SB, with MC K4, with CC1 SB, with MC K6, with CC1 SB, with MC K4, with CC1 SB, with MC K7]; repeat from * 2 more times, end [with CC1 SB, with MC K4, with CC1 SB, with MC K6, with CC1 SB, with MC K4, with CC1, SB, with MC K4]. Cut CC1.

Round 3: With MC, K6, * [with CC2 work BB using horizontal bar between stitches, with MC K12, with CC2 BB as before, with MC K13]; repeat from * 2 more times, end [with CC2 work BB as before, with MC K12, with CC2 work BB as before, with MC K7]. Cut CC2.

Round 4: As Round 2.

Round 5: As Round 1. Cut CC1.

ALL SIZES, AFTER COMPLETING FLOWERS

Knit every round with MC, until body of hat measures 2 (3, 4)"/5 (7.5, 10) cm from ridge.

BOTTOM EDGE

Knit 1 round.

Purl 3 rounds for ridge.

Knit 1 round.

Work a (K1, P1) rib for approximately 1"/2.5 cm.

Cast off in rib. You may want to use a 4.5mm/ US7 needle to cast off for a looser edge.

FINISH

Tie the I-cord at the top into a knot to look like a Big centre Bobble and tack down with cast on tail. Sew in ends.

Block and enjoy!

CARNIVAL COAT

Experience Level: With Gusto!
(Enthusiastic Beginner)

adapted by Lynda Gemmell

ABBREVIATIONS:

Garter Stitch: Knit every row.

K2tog: Right slanting decrease: Knit the next two stitches together.

Kfb: Increase of 1 stitch: Knit into the front of the next stitch as usual and without taking the stitch off the left needle, knit into the back of the same stitch.

pm: Place a marker.

SL1: Slip one stitch.

sm: Slip the marker.

SSK: Left leaning decrease: Slip the next stitch as if to knit, slip the next stitch as if to knit, insert the left needle into the fronts of the two slipped stitches on the right needle. Knit the 2 slipped stitches together.

Stocking Stitch: Knit 1 row (RS), purl 1 row.

yo: Yarn over to make a hole (eyelet) and increase one stitch: Bring wool under the right needle and forward to the front of your work, swing the wool over the right needle to the back of your work ready to work the next stitch. The resulting loop is purled in the next row.

This bright coat is worked using a very bright variegated yarn. It will work equally well using two solid colours or a "quieter" variegated or hand-painted yarn.

Why not try several versions!

Needles:

Two x 4.0mm/US6 circular needle (24"/60 cm long)
4.0mm/US6 double-point needles

Tension:

Stocking Stitch:

22 stitches = 4"/10 cm on 4.0mm/US6 needle in stocking stitch or needle needed to obtain this tension.

Garter Stitch for skirt only:

20 stitches = 4"/10 cm on 4.0mm/US6 needle in garter stitch or needle needed to obtain this tension.

Directions are given for size 1, other sizes are in brackets. If only one figure is shown, it applies to all sizes.

To Fit:	1 year	2 year	4 year	6 year
Chest Size of:	20"	22"	24"	26"
	51 cm	56 cm	61 cm	66 cm
Finished Size:				
Chest	24"	26"	29"	31"
	61 cm	66 cm	73.5 cm	79 cm
Sleeve Length	6½"	8"	10"	12"
	16.5 cm	20.5 cm	25.5 cm	30.5 cm
Body Length	12"	13"	15"	17"
	30.5 cm	33 cm	38 cm	43 cm

Materials: DK Yarn - 50g ball, 119m/130yds

	1 year	2 year	4 year	6 year
Main Colour	2	3	3	4
Contrast Colour:				
Option 1:	2	2.5	3	3
Option 2 (stripes):	2	2	2	3
Ring markers	6	6	6	6
Big Buttons 1¼" / 3 cm	2	2	3	3
2-hole shirt buttons	2	2	3	3

Buttonhole twist thread

The sample followed Option #2: (worked in stripes) and is a Size 1 with 2 buttons. All other sizes have 3 buttons. This sample is knit in Emu Superwash wool in colours Purple #3633 and Carnival #218.

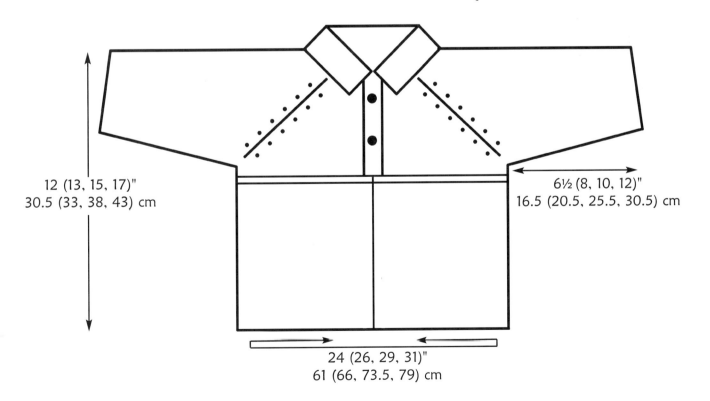

12 (13, 15, 17)"
30.5 (33, 38, 43) cm

6½ (8, 10, 12)"
16.5 (20.5, 25.5, 30.5) cm

24 (26, 29, 31)"
61 (66, 73.5, 79) cm

This coat has two colour options:

To make things easier, OPTION 1 uses only the variegated colour in the garter stitch collar, cuffs and skirt.

In OPTION 2, the Main Colour and the variegated colour alternate for garter stitch stripes in the collar, cuffs and skirt.

Construction Notes: The increase used in the sample on page 84 is a Yarn Over (yo).

BEGIN AT THE COLLAR

COLLAR OPTION 1: (WORKED IN CC)

With Contrast Colour (CC), Cast On 64 (72, 78, 84) stitches.

Work back and forth on the circular needle in Garter Stitch (knit every row) for 2½ (3, 3, 3¼)"/6.5 (7.5, 7.5, 8) cm, ending after a RS row. Break CC yarn. Continue with Collar Shaping below.

COLLAR OPTION 2: (WORKED IN STRIPES)

With Main Colour (MC), Cast On 64 (72, 78, 84) stitches.

Work back and forth on the circular needle in Garter Stitch (knit every row), as follows:

Next Row: (WS) With MC, knit.

> **Garter Stitch Stripes:**
>
> Knit 2 rows with Contrast Colour (CC) (makes 1 ridge on RS).
> Knit 2 rows with MC (makes 1 ridge).

Work Garter Stitch Stripes alternating the MC and CC every two rows, for 2½ (3, 3, 3¼)"/6 (7.5, 7.5, 8) cm, ending after a WS row. Break CC yarn.

Next Row: (RS) With MC, knit.

Continue with Collar Shaping below.

COLLAR SHAPING - BOTH OPTIONS

Row 1: With Main Colour (MC) and WS facing, K4, [K2tog] 28 (32, 35, 38) times, K4. (36, 40, 43, 46 sts)

Row 2: (RS) K4, P28 (32, 35, 38), K4.

Row 3: Knit.

Row 4: K4, P28 (32, 35, 38), K4.

Row 5: K4, [knit into the front and back (Kfb) of next stitch] 28 (32, 35, 38) times, K4. (64, 72, 78, 84 sts)

Row 6: K4, P56 (64, 70, 76), K4.

Note: This collar is flipped over when worn so that the even numbered rows are showing when the sweater is on. The RS for the rest of the coat is indicated in the instructions.

YOKE

We are now going to set up 4 shapelines for the raglan shoulder shaping. Markers will be set between the 2 knit stitches of the shapelines. Eyelet yarn over increases will be worked before and after each of the shapelines. Stitches for the button bands are also added now.

LET'S BEGIN

Row 1: (RS) With Main Colour, Cast On 8 stitches (for left button band), knit these 8 stitches, place marker (pm), K10 (12, 13, 14) stitches for left Front, yo, K1, pm, K1, yo, K8 (8, 9, 10) stitches for sleeve, yo, K1, pm, K1, yo, K20 (24, 26, 28) stitches for Back, yo, K1, pm, K1, yo, K8 (8, 9, 10) stitches for sleeve, yo, K1, pm, K1, yo, K10 (12, 13, 14) stitches for right Front.

Row 2: Cast On 8 stitches (right button band), knit these 8 stitches, pm, purl to last marker, purling loops of yo increases, K8. (88, 96, 102, 108 sts)

Row 3: (RS) K8, slip marker (sm), *knit to 1 stitch before next marker, yo, K1, sm, K1, yo; repeat from * 3 more times, knit to end of row. (increase of 8 stitches-96, 104, 110, 116 sts)

Row 4: K8, purl to last 8 stitches, K8.

Repeat Rows 3 & 4, 4 (4, 1, 2) more times (increasing at the shapeline markers as set).

Buttonholes are now placed on both the right and left buttonbands. The buttons will be sewn over the holes on the appropriate buttonband, which ensures that the buttons and the buttonholes will line up perfectly.

Buttonhole Row: (RS) K4, Cast Off 3 stitches, sm, continue in pattern working the increases as set to the last marker, sm, K1, Cast Off 3 stitches, K3.

Next Row: (WS) K4, Cast On 3 stitches, K1, purl to last marker, sm, K1, Cast On 3 stitches, K4.

Continue to Repeat Rows 3 & 4 above, increasing as set, making buttonholes after every 10 (9, 10, 11) garter stitch ridges (every 20, 18, 20, 22 rows). The buttonholes will sit between the ridges.

Continue until you can count 20 (22, 24, 26) pairs of eyelets along the raglan shapelines, ending after a WS row. (240, 264, 286, 308 sts)

Don't forget your buttonholes! (The two smallest sizes will have 2 buttonholes, the 2 larger sizes have 3 buttonholes.)

Work 2 rows even without increases, ending after a WS row.

SLEEVES

We now have 2 methods for completing the sleeves.

1) Working the sleeves in the round on double-point needles, with "no sew" finishing.

2) Working the sleeve stitches back and forth on the circular needle and sewing up the sleeve seam.

It's your choice!

SLEEVE METHOD 1: IN THE ROUND.

DIVIDE Body and first Sleeve: (RS) Knit across 39 (43, 46, 49) stitches of left Front ; knit next 50 (54, 59, 64) stitches onto double-point needles for the sleeve, dividing these stitches evenly on the needles.

Join sleeve stitches in the round, place marker at beginning of the round.

Knit 5 (5, 7, 7) rounds.

Decrease Round: K1, K2tog, knit to last 3 stitches, SSK, K1.

Repeat last 6 (6, 8, 8) rounds until sleeve measures 5½ (7, 9, 11)"/14 (18, 23, 28) cm from dividing row.

CUFF - Work the Option of your choice

CUFF Option 1: (worked in CC)

With CC, Knit 1 round.

Next Round: Purl, decreasing evenly to 38 (38, 39, 40) stitches, if necessary.

Next Round: Knit.

Next Round: Purl.

Repeat last two rounds until there are 5 (5, 6, 6) garter stitch ridges, ending with a knit round.

With RS facing, **Cast Off** while purling.

CUFF Option 2: (worked in stripes)

Next Round: With MC, purl, decreasing evenly to 38 (38, 39, 40) stitches, if necessary.

Next Round: With CC knit.

Next Round: With CC purl.

Next Round: With MC knit.

Next Round: With MC purl.

Repeat the last four rounds until there are 5 (5, 6, 6) garter stitch ridges, ending with a knit round.

With RS facing, **Cast Off** while purling.

BOTH OPTIONS, Continue for Second Sleeve:

Divide for second sleeve: Attach MC yarn and knit across 62 (70, 76, 82) stitches to next marker, knit 50 (54, 59, 64) stitches for next sleeve onto double-point needles, dividing equally among the double-point needles.

Work same as first sleeve.

Finish Dividing Row: Attach MC yarn and knit remaining stitches from right Front. (140, 156, 168, 180 stitches on circular needle for Body)

Continue with BODY.

SLEEVE METHOD 2: WORKED FLAT.

DIVIDE Body and Sleeve: (RS) Knit across 39 (43, 46, 49) stitches of Front; knit next 50 (54, 59, 64) stitches of sleeve, Turn.

Next Row: P50 (54, 59, 64) stitches for sleeve.

Working back and forth on sleeve stitches, work 4 (4, 6, 6) rows in Stocking Stitch.

Decrease Row: (RS) K1, K2tog, knit to last 3 stitches, SSK, K1.

Work 5 (5, 7, 7) rows in Stocking Stitch.

Repeat last 6 (6, 8, 8) rows until sleeve measures 5½ (7, 9, 11)"/14 (18, 23, 28) cm from dividing row, ending after a WS row.

CUFF - WORK THE OPTION OF YOUR CHOICE

CUFF Option 1: (worked in CC)

Next Row: (RS) With CC, Knit 1 row.

Next Row: Knit, decreasing evenly to 38 (38, 39, 40) stitches, if necessary.

Knit every row until there are 5 (5, 6, 6) garter stitch ridges, ending with a WS row. With RS facing, **Cast Off** while purling.

CUFF Option 2: (worked in stripes)

Next Row: (RS) With MC, knit, decreasing evenly to 38 (38, 39, 40) stitches, if necessary.

Next Row: With MC, knit.

Next Row: (RS) With CC, knit.

Next Row: With CC, knit.

Next Row: (RS) With MC, knit.

Next Row: With MC, knit.

Repeat last 4 rows until there are 5 (5, 6, 6) garter stitch ridges. With RS facing, **Cast Off** while purling.

BOTH OPTIONS, Continue for Second Sleeve:

Divide for second Sleeve: Attach MC yarn and knit across 62 (70, 76, 82) stitches of Back to next marker; knit next 50 (54, 59, 64) stitches for sleeve, Turn.

Work as for first sleeve.

Finish Dividing Row: Attach yarn and knit remaining stitches of right Front to end of row. (140, 156, 168, 180 sts on circular needle for Body)

The sample below followed Option #1 (worked in Contrast Colour) and is knit in Emu Superwash wool in colours Red #4 and Carnival #218.

Carnival Coat

BODY

Next Row: (WS) With MC, K8, purl to first sleeve junction, pick up 2 stitches to close gaps, purl to next sleeve junction, pick up 2 stitches, purl to last 8 stitches, K8.

Next Row: (RS) Knit to extra underarm stitches, K2tog, knit to extra underarm stitches, K2tog, knit to end of row. (142, 158, 170, 182 sts)

GARTER STITCH RIDGES

RIDGE OPTION 1: (WORKED IN CC)

Next Row: (WS) With MC, K8, purl to last 8 stitches, K8.

Next Row: (RS) With CC, knit, decreasing 8 (8, 12, 12) stitches evenly across row. (134, 150, 158, 170 sts.)

Knit 2 more rows with CC, ending after working a RS row. (1 CC ridge showing on RS)

Set aside Yoke, leaving stitches on circular needle.

RIDGE OPTION 2: (WORKED IN STRIPES)

Next Row: (WS) With MC knit, decreasing 8 (8, 12, 12) stitches evenly across the row as follows: decrease 2 (2, 3, 3) stitches evenly across the Front, 4 (4, 6, 6) evenly across the Back, and 2 (2, 3, 3) across the other Front. (134, 150, 158, 170 sts)

Next Row: (RS) With CC, knit.

Next Row: With CC Knit. Break CC yarn.

Next Row: (RS) With MC, knit.

Set aside Yoke, leaving sts on circular needle.

SKIRT

SKIRT OPTION 1: (WORKED IN CC)

With another circular needle of same size:

With CC, Cast On 30 (37, 43, 50) stitches.

Row 1: Knit.

Knit every row until you have 133 (149, 157, 169) ridges.

Next Row: Knit.

Cast Off knitways. (total of 134, 150, 158, 170 ridges, including the cast off ridge)

SKIRT OPTION 2: (WORKED IN STRIPES)

With another circular needle of same size:

With MC, Cast On 30 (37, 43, 50) stitches.

Next Row: With MC, Knit.

Row 1: With CC, knit.

Row 2: With CC, knit.

Row 3: With MC, knit.

Row 4: With MC, knit.

Repeat last four rows until you have 133 (149, 157, 169) Ridges.

Next Row: With next colour in sequence, knit.

Cast Off knitways. (134, 150, 158, 170 ridges, including the cast off ridge)

JOIN SKIRT - BOTH OPTIONS.

With circular needle and RS facing, pick up and knit 1 stitch for every Garter Stitch Ridge using the following colours:

Note: Pick up stitches along whichever edge looks less neat.

Option 1: Use CC yarn.

Option 2: Use MC yarn.

Note: This should give you 134 (150, 158, 170) sts to match the number of stitches on your yoke.

You are now going to join the yoke and the skirt together using the Three Needle Cast Off technique. This will give a tidy join and mimic the Garter Stitch ridges.

With both WS's facing together, (work on the RS of the sweater), using a double-pointed needle of the same size, for your third working needle, work a **3 Needle Cast Off** to end (see page 102 for 3 Needle Cast Off instructions).

FINISHING

Sew sleeve seams if necessary, closing gap at underarm.

Weave in ends.

Sew buttons over the buttonholes on the Left Band for girls or Right Band for boys.

Block if necessary.

TEXTURE TIME

Experience Level: With Gusto!
(Enthusiastic Beginner)

adapted by Deb Gemmell

ABBREVIATIONS:

Inc 1: Increase 1 stitch. See Increases at the end of the book for descriptions of various increase methods.

K2tog: Right slanting decrease. Knit the next two stitches together.

Kfb: Increase of 1 stitch: Knit into the front of the next stitch as usual and without taking the stitch off the left needle, knit into the back of the same stitch.

M1: Make one stitch (no holes). With the left needle lift the running thread between the stitch just worked and the next stitch, from front to back, and knit into the back of the resulting loop.

pm: Place a marker.

sm: Slip the marker.

SSK: Left leaning decrease. Slip the next stitch as if to knit, slip the next stitch as if to knit, insert the left needle into the fronts of the two slipped stitches on the right needle. Knit the 2 slipped stitches together.

A combination of Garter Stitch and Broken Rib patterns make for an appealing sweater with a tactile texture.

Needles:

4.0mm/US6 circular needle (24"/60 cm long)

Tension:

22 stitches = 4"/10 cm on 4.0mm/US6 needle in stocking stitch or needle needed to obtain this tension.

Directions are given for size 1, other sizes are in brackets. If only one figure is shown, it applies to all sizes.

Sample left, was worked in Patons Bumble Bee cotton in colour #80731. Sample below, in Emu machine washable wool, Walnut Print #8.

To Fit:	1 year	2 year	4 year	6 year
Chest Size of:	20"	22"	24"	26"
	51 cm	56 cm	61 cm	66 cm
Finished Size:				
Chest	24"	26"	29"	31"
	61 cm	66 cm	74 cm	79 cm
Sleeve Length	6½"	8"	10"	12"
	16.5 cm	20.5 cm	25.5 cm	30.5 cm
Body Length	12"	13"	15"	17"
	30.5 cm	33 cm	38 cm	43 cm

Materials: DK Yarn - 50g ball, 119m/130yds

Main Colour	4	5	6	7
Ring markers	10	10	10	10
Shank Buttons (15mm)	5	6	6	7
Shirt Buttons (2-hole)	5	6	6	7

Buttonhole twist thread

BEGIN AT THE COLLAR

Cast On 65 (73, 77, 85) stitches.

Work back and forth on the circular needle, in Garter Stitch (knit every row), for 2½ (3, 3, 3¼)"/6.5 (7.5, 7.5, 8) cm, ending after a RS row.

COLLAR SHAPING

Row 1: With WS facing, K4, [K2tog] 14 (16, 17, 19) times, K1, [K2tog] 14 (16, 17, 19) times, K4. (37, 41, 43, 47 sts)

Row 2: (RS) K4, P29 (33, 35, 39), K4.

Row 3: Knit.

Row 4: K4, P29 (33, 35, 39), K4.

Row 5: K4, [knit into the front and back (Kfb) of next stitch] 14 (16, 17, 19) times, K1, [Kfb] 14 (16, 17, 19) times, K4. (65, 73, 77, 85 sts)

Row 6: K4, P57 (65, 69, 77), K4.

Note: This collar is flipped over when worn so that the even numbered rows are showing when the sweater is on. The RS for the rest of the jacket is indicated in the instructions.

YOKE

We are now going to set up 4 shapelines for the raglan shoulder shaping. A marker will be set before and after each of the 2 stitch shapelines and another marker also delineates the buttonbands on the Fronts. Use any of the closed increases.

Stitches for the button bands are added in the next 2 rows.

LET'S BEGIN

SET-UP Pattern Row: (RS) Cast On 5 stitches (for left button band), knit these 5 stitches, place marker (pm). Continue across row as follows:

Front:	[K1, P1] 5 (5, 6, 7) times, K1;
Shapeline 1:	pm, K2, pm;
Sleeve:	[K1, P1] 3 (4, 4, 4) times, K1;
Shapeline 2:	pm, K2, pm;
Back:	[K1, P1] 10 (12, 12, 14) times, K1;
Shapeline 3:	pm, K2, pm;
Sleeve:	[K1, P1] 3 (4, 4, 4) times, K1,
Shapeline 4:	pm, K2, pm,
Front:	[K1, P1] 5 (5, 6, 7) times, K1. (70, 78, 82, 90 sts)

SET-UP Increase Row: Cast on 5 stitches (right button band), knit these 5 stitches, pm, *knit to shapeline marker, M1, slip marker (sm), K2, sm, M1; repeat from * for next 3 shapelines, knit across the Front to last marker and K5 for buttonband. (83, 91, 95, 103 sts)

Pattern Row 1: (RS) Work across Row as follows:

Buttonband:	K5, sm;
Front:	work [K1, P1] to next marker;
Shapeline 1:	sm, K2, sm;
Sleeve:	P1, work [K1, P1] to next marker;
Shapeline 2:	sm, K2, sm;
Back:	P1, work [K1, P1] to next marker;
Shapeline 3:	sm, K2, sm;
Sleeve:	P1, work [K1, P1] to next marker;
Shapeline4:	sm, K2, sm;
Front:	P1, work [K1, P1], ending with a K1 at next marker;
Buttonband:	sm, K5.

Increase Row 2: K5, sm, *knit to next marker, M1, sm, K2, sm, M1; repeat from * for next 3 shapelines, knit to last marker and K5. (increase of 8 stitches - 91, 99, 103, 111 sts)

Pattern Row 3: (RS) Work across row as follows:

Buttonband:	K5, sm;
Front:	work [K1, P1] to marker, ending with a K1;
Shapeline 1:	pm, K2, pm;
Sleeve:	work [K1, P1] to marker, ending with a K1;
Shapeline 2:	pm, K2, pm;
Back:	work [K1, P1] to marker, ending with a K1;
Shapeline 3:	pm, K2, pm;
Sleeve:	work [K1, P1] to marker, ending with a K1;
Shapeline 4:	pm, K2, pm

Front: work [K1, P1] to marker, ending with a K1;

Buttonband: sm, K5.

Increase Row 4: K5, sm, *knit to next marker, M1, sm, K2, sm, M1; repeat from * for next 3 shapelines, knit to last marker and K5. (99, 107, 111, 119 sts)

Repeat Rows 1 & 2 once more. (107, 115, 119, 127 sts)

Buttonholes are now placed on both the right and left buttonbands. The buttons will be sewn over the holes on the appropriate buttonband, which ensures that the buttons and the buttonholes will line up perfectly.

Repeat Row 3, working Make Buttonholes (see box) in 5 stitches of buttonband at beginning and end of row.

Make Buttonholes: (RS) K2, K2tog, yo, K1, sm, work pattern for appropriate Row to last marker, sm, K1, yo, K2tog, K2.

Repeat Increase Row 4.

Repeat Rows 1 - 4, increasing as set, making buttonholes after every 9 (10, 10, 10) garter stitch ridges (every 18, 20, 20, 20 rows). The buttonholes will sit between the ridges.

Work until there are 219 (243, 263, 287) stitches on needle, ending after an Increase Row.

---

*Note: All the **Pattern Rounds** can be worked as follows:*

Pattern Round: (RS) K5, sm, [K1, P1] to shapeline marker, *take note of last stitch worked (could be either a K1 or a P1), sm, K2, sm, mirror across the shapeline and begin the rib pattern with the same stitch as last worked before the shapeline, rib to next marker; repeat from * at next three shapelines, mirror across last shapeline , rib across the Front, sm, K5.

GARTER STITCH STRIP

Knit every row until there are 2 (3, 3, 3) ridges showing on RS, ending after a WS row.

Don't forget your buttonholes!

SLEEVES

Designers Note: I recommend working the sleeves flat. It seems easier to work the sleeves and takes but a moment to sew up the garter stitch seam.

SLEEVES

Divide Body and Sleeve: (RS) K5, sm, K29 (31, 35, 39) stitches of Front to marker, remove marker, K1 of the shapeline stitches; the next 45 (51, 55, 59) stitches are for the sleeve and worked as follows, K1 shapeline stitch, remove marker, K43 (49, 53, 57) stitches to next marker, remove marker, K1 shapeline stitch, Turn.

Work back and forth on circular needle for sleeve, as follows:

Next Row: K45 (51, 55, 59) sts for sleeve, Turn.

Repeat last row until 2 more ridges showing on RS, ending after a RS row.

Next Row: (WS) Knit across increasing 4 stitches evenly. (49, 55, 59, 63 sts) - 3 ridges showing on RS.

Establish Pattern: (RS) K6 (9, 10, 12), place marker, [K1, P1] 18 (18, 19, 19) times, K1, place marker, K6 (9, 10, 12).

Next Row: (WS) Knit.

TAPER THE SLEEVE

Pattern Row 1: (RS) Knit to marker, sm, work [K1, P1] across 37 (37, 39, 39) sts of sleeve to next marker ending with a K1, sm, knit to end of row.

Row 2: (WS) Knit.

Repeat Rows 1 & 2 - 1 (1, 2, 2) more times.

Decrease Row: (RS) Knit to 2 sts before marker, K2tog, slip marker, work in pattern to next marker, slip marker, SSK, knit to end of row.

Next Row: (WS) Knit.

Repeat last 6 (6, 8, 8) rows until sleeve has 41 (41, 43, 43) sts.

Continue working in pattern with no further decreases until sleeve measures 5½ (7, 9, 11)"/14

(18, 23, 28) cm from dividing row, ending after a WS row.

Next Row: Knit, decreasing 3 stitches. (38, 38, 40, 40) sts

Knit every row until 5 ridges showing on RS, ending after a RS row.

With WS facing, **Cast Off** knitwise. Cut yarn.

Divide for second Sleeve: Attach yarn and with RS facing, K1, remove marker, K57 (65, 69, 77) sts of Back to next marker, remove marker, K1; second sleeve as follows, K1, K43 (49, 53, 57) sts, K1, Turn.

Work as for first sleeve.

Finish Dividing Row: Attach yarn and knit remaining stitches of right Front to end of row. (129, 141, 153, 169 sts on circular needle for Body)

BODY

Don't Forget to work Buttonholes!

You may wish to sew up the sleeve seams now.

Row 1: (WS) K5, knit to first sleeve junction, pick up 2 sts to close gaps, knit to next sleeve junction, pick up 2 sts, knit to last 5 sts, K5.

Row 2: K5, sm, *knit to extra underarm sts, K2tog; repeat once, knit to end of row. (131, 143, 155, 171 sts)

Row 3: Knit.

Row 4: Knit.

Increase 8 stitches around the sweater in the next row as follows:

Row 5: (WS) Knit, increasing 2 stitches in the Front, increasing 4 stitches across the Back, increasing 2 stitches across the Front. (139, 151, 163, 179 sts)

ESTABLISH PATTERN

Pattern Row 1: (RS) K5, work [K1, P1] rib to last 6 stitches, ending with a K6.

Row 2: (WS) Knit.

Repeat last 2 rows, continuing to work buttonholes every 9 (10, 10, 10) garter stitch ridges, until sweater measures 11 (12, 14, 16)"/28 (30.5, 35.5, 40.5) cm, ending after a WS row. Measure from the base of the collar (collar is not included in this measurement) down the centre back of the sweater to your needle. You can lengthen the sweater here and work to desired finished length.

Decrease Row: K10, K2tog, work [K8, K2tog] to last 9 (11, 13, 9) stitches, knit to end of row.

Knit every row until 5 ridges are showing on the RS.

With WS facing, **Cast Off** knitways.

FINISHING

Sew sleeve seams, closing gap at underarm.

Weave in ends.

Sew buttons over the buttonholes on the Left Band for girls or Right Band for boys.

Block if necessary.

Sewing a Garter Stitch Seam

Looking at the right sides of the sleeves, align the side seams so the garter stitch bumps line up. To sew the seam insert a blunt sewing-up needle into the garter stitch bump on one side and then into the bump of the corresponding stitch on the other side. Continue sewing up the garter stitch bumps, alternating from one side to the other.

CALYPSO JACKET

Experience Level: Intermediate

designed by Dana Gibbons

Abbreviations:

Garter Stitch: Knit every row.

Stocking Stitch: Knit 1 row (RS), purl 1 row.

K2tog: Right slanting decrease: Knit the next two stitches together.

Kfb: Increase of 1 stitch: Knit into the front of the next stitch as usual and without taking the stitch off the left needle, knit into the back of the same stitch.

pm: Place a marker.

SL1: Slip one stitch purlwise.

sm: Slip the marker.

SSK: Left leaning decrease: Slip the next stitch as if to knit, slip the next stitch as if to knit, insert the left needle into the fronts of the two slipped stitches on the right needle. Knit the 2 slipped stitches together.

yo: Yarn over to make a hole (eyelet) and increase one stitch: Bring wool under the right needle and forward to the front of your work, swing the wool over the right needle to the back of your work ready to knit the next stitch. The resulting loop is purled in the next row.

The Calypso Jacket, as shown, is bright and cheerful in five different colours for fun days out. It can also be knit using only three colours as shown on page 17. To obtain this effect, use one colour for both CC1 & CC3, use a second contrast colour for CC2 & CC4.

Needles:

4.0mm/US6 circular needle (24"/60 cm long)
4.0mm/US6 double-point needles (for "no sew" sleeves)

Tension:

22 stitches = 4"/10 cm on 4.0mm/US6 needle in stocking stitch or needle needed to obtain this tension.

Directions are given for size 1, other sizes are in brackets. If only one figure is shown, it applies to all sizes.

The Calypso Jacket is knit in Butterfly Super 10 cotton. The Main Colour is Peony #3459 and the Contrast Colours are: Canary #3553, Azure #3062, Lime #3724 and Nectarine #3402.

To Fit:	1 year	2 year	4 year	6 year
Chest Size of:	20"	22"	24"	26"
	51 cm	56 cm	61 cm	66 cm
Finished Size:				
Chest	24"	26"	29"	31"
	61 cm	66 cm	73.5 cm	79 cm
Sleeve Length	6½"	8"	10"	12"
	16.5 cm	20.5 cm	25.5 cm	30.5 cm
Body Length	12"	13"	15"	17"
	30.5 cm	33 cm	38 cm	43 cm

Materials: DK Yarn - 125g skeins, 230m/250yds

Sweater:

Main Colour	1½	2	2	2½
Contrast Colour 1	½	½	½	1
Contrast Colour 2	¼	½	½	½
Contrast Colour 3	¼	¼	¼	¼
Contrast Colour 4	¼	¼	¼	¼
Ring markers	6	6	6	6
Shank Buttons (15mm)	5	6	6	7
Shirt Buttons (2-hole)	5	6	6	7

Buttonhole twist thread

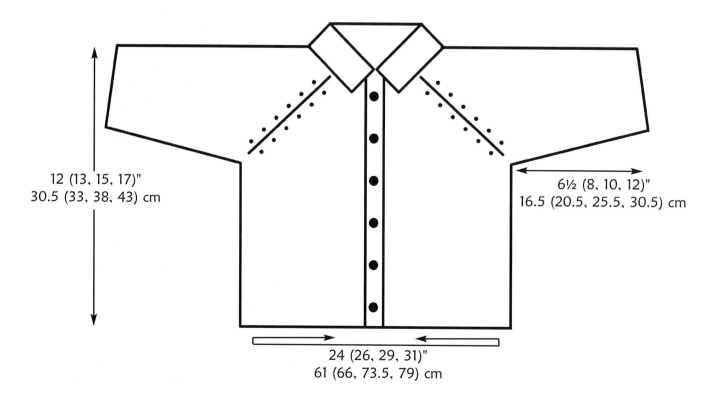

12 (13, 15, 17)"
30.5 (33, 38, 43) cm

6½ (8, 10, 12)"
16.5 (20.5, 25.5, 30.5) cm

24 (26, 29, 31)"
61 (66, 73.5, 79) cm

BEGIN AT THE COLLAR

With Main Colour (MC) **Cast On** 64 (72, 78, 84) stitches.

Work back and forth on the circular needle, in Garter Stitch (knit every row), for 2½ (3, 3, 3¼) "/6.5 (7.5, 7.5, 8) cm, ending after a RS row.

COLLAR SHAPING

Row 1: With WS facing, K4, [K2tog] 28 (32, 35, 38) times, K4. (36, 40, 43, 46 sts)

Row 2: (RS) K4, P28 (32, 35, 38), K4.

Row 3: Knit.

Row 4: K4, P28 (32, 35, 38), K4.

Row 5: K4, [knit into the front and back (Kfb) of next stitch] 28 (32, 35, 38) times, K4. (64, 72, 78, 84 sts)

Row 6: K4, P56 (64, 70, 76), K4.

Note: *This collar is flipped over when worn so that the even numbered rows are showing when the sweater is on. The RS for the rest of the jacket is indicated in the instructions.*

YOKE

We are now going to set up 4 shapelines for the raglan shoulder shaping. Markers will be set between the 2 knit stitches of the shapelines. Stitches for the button bands are also added now.

Buttonholes will be placed on both the right and left buttonbands. The buttons will be sewn over the holes on the appropriate buttonband, which ensures that the buttons and the button-holes will line up perfectly.

LET'S BEGIN

Set-Up Row: (RS) Cast On 5 stitches (for left button band), knit these 5 stitches, K10 (12, 13, 14) stitches for left Front, yo, K1, pm, K1, yo, K8 (8, 9, 10) stitches for sleeve, yo, K1, pm, K1, yo, K20 (24, 26, 28) stitches for Back, yo, K1, pm, K1, yo, K8 (8, 9, 10) stitches for sleeve, yo, K1, pm, K1, yo, K10 (12, 13, 14) stitches for right Front.

Set-Up Row: Cast on 5 stitches (right button band), knit these 5 stitches, purl to last marker,

purling loops of yo increases, K5. (82, 90, 96, 102 sts)

Increase Row 1: (RS) K5, *knit to 1 stitch before next marker, yo, K1, sm, K1, yo; repeat from * 3 more times, knit to end of row. (increase of 8 stitches - 90, 98, 104, 110 sts)

Straight Row 2: K5, purl to last 5 stitches, K5.

Size 6 ONLY: Repeat Rows 1 & 2 once more (increasing at shapeline markers as set).

All Sizes:

Work the GARTER STRIPES PATTERN in box.

GARTER STRIPE PATTERN

Maintain buttonbands in MC throughout pattern. Work the right buttonband with a separate ball or bobbin of MC for the 4 rows of Ridge Stripes below and then return to working with one MC ball. Twist colours ON WRONG SIDE OF SWEATER by picking up the new colour from under the old colour.

Increase Row 1: (RS) With MC, K5, with CC1, *knit to 1 stitch before next marker, yo, K1, sm, K1, yo; repeat from * 3 more times, knit to last 5 sts, with MC K5.

Ridge Row 2: With MC K5, with CC1 knit to last 5 sts, with MC K5.

Buttonhole Row 3: (RS) With MC, K1, K2tog, yo, K2, *with CC2, knit to 1 st before next marker, yo, K1, sm, K1, yo; repeat from * 3 more times, knit to last 5 sts, with MC, K2, yo, K2tog, K1.

Ridge Row 4: With MC, K5, with CC2 knit to last 5 sts, with MC, K5.

The buttonholes will sit between the 2 coloured ridges.

Change to Main Colour.

Increase Row 5: (RS) With MC, K5, *knit to 1 stitch before next marker, yo, K1, sm, K1, yo; repeat from * 3 more times, knit to end of row.

Straight Row 6: With MC, K5, purl to last 5 sts, K5.

Repeat Rows 5 and 6, 5 (6, 7, 7) more times (total of 12, 14, 16, 16 rows in MC).

Repeat Garter Stripe Pattern, until you can count 20 (22, 24, 26) pairs of eyelets along the raglan shapelines, ending after a WS row. (234, 258, 280, 302 sts)

Work 2 rows even without increases, ending after a WS row.

SLEEVES

We now have 2 methods for completing the sleeves.

1) Working the sleeves in the round on double-point needles, with "no sew" finishing.

2) Working the sleeve stitches back and forth on the circular needle and sewing up the sleeve seam.

It's your choice!

SLEEVE METHOD 1: IN THE ROUND.

Divide Body and first Sleeve: (RS) With MC, knit across 36 (40, 43, 46) stitches of left Front; knit next 50 (54, 59, 64) stitches onto double-point needles for the sleeve, dividing these stitches evenly on the needles.

Join sleeve stitches in the round, place marker at beginning of the round.

Continue to work in the row sequence of GARTER STRIPE Pattern as before, but note that MC rounds are knit and CC Stripes are worked as below, see box.

AT THE SAME TIME - work a Decrease Round every 6 (8, 8, 8) rounds.

Decrease Round: (RS) K1, K2tog, knit to last 3 stitches, SSK, K1.

GARTER STRIPE PATTERN - in the round:

Round 1: (RS) With CC1, knit.

Ridge Round 2: (RS) With CC1, purl. Break CC1. (makes a ridge)

Round 3: With CC2, knit.

Ridge Round 4: With CC2, purl. Break CC2. (makes a ridge)

Change to Main Colour.

With MC, knit 12 (14, 16, 16) rounds.

Continue until sleeve measures 5½ (7, 9, 11)"/14 (18, 23, 28) cm from dividing row.

Next Round: With MC, purl, decreasing evenly to 38 (38, 39, 40) stitches, if necessary.

Next Round: Knit.

Next Round: Purl.

Repeat last 2 rounds until there are 5 (5, 6, 6) garter stitch ridges, ending with a knit round.

With RS facing, **Cast Off** while purling.

Divide for second sleeve: Attach MC yarn and knit across 62 (70, 76, 82) stitches to next marker, knit 50 (54, 59, 64) stitches for next sleeve onto double-point needles, dividing equally among the double-point needles.

Work same as first sleeve.

Finish Dividing Row: Attach MC yarn and knit remaining stitches from right Front. (134, 150, 162, 174 sts on circular needle for Body)

SLEEVE METHOD 2: WORKED FLAT.

Divide Body and Sleeve: (RS) With MC, knit across 36 (40, 43, 46) stitches of Front; knit next 50 (54, 59, 64) stitches of sleeve, Turn.

Row 2: P50 (54, 59, 64) stitches for sleeve.

Work back and forth on sleeve stitches.

Continue to work GARTER STRIPE Pattern and follow changes for sleeve worked FLAT (see box on next page).

AT THE SAME TIME - work a Decrease Row every 6 (8, 8, 8) rounds.

Decrease Row: (RS) K1, K2tog, knit to last 3 stitches, SSK, K1.

GARTER STRIPE PATTERN - worked FLAT:

Row 1: (RS) With CC1, knit.

Ridge Row 2: (WS) With CC1, knit. Break CC1 (makes a ridge).

Row 3: With CC2, knit.

Ridge Row 4: With CC2, knit. Break CC2 (makes a ridge).

Change to Main Colour.

With MC, work 12 (14, 16, 16) rows in stocking stitch.

Continue until sleeve measures 5½ (7, 9, 11)"/14 (18, 23, 28) cm from dividing row, ending after a RS row.

Next Row: (WS) With MC, knit, decreasing evenly to 38 (38, 39, 40) stitches, if necessary.

Knit every row until there are 5 (5, 6, 6) garter stitch ridges showing on the RS, end after knitting a RS row.

With WS facing, **Cast Off** knitwise. Cut yarn.

Divide for second Sleeve: Attach MC yarn and knit across 62 (70, 76, 82) stitches of Back to next marker; knit next 50 (54, 59, 64) stitches for sleeve, Turn.

Work as for first sleeve.

Finish Dividing Row: Attach MC yarn and knit remaining stitches of right Front to end of row. (134, 150, 162, 174 sts on circular needle for Body)

BODY

Next Row: (WS) With MC, K5, purl to first sleeve junction, pick up 2 stitches to close gaps, purl to next sleeve junction, pick up 2 stitches, purl to last 5 stitches, K5.

Set-Up for Pattern:

Next Row: (RS) Knit to extra underarm stitches, K2tog, Knit to centre of Back, Inc 1 stitch, knit to extra underarm stitches, K2tog, knit to end of row. (137, 153, 165, 177 sts)

Next Row: Knit.

Note: Maintain the buttonbands in Main Colour throughout, by using separate Main Colour balls or wind 2 Main Colour bobbins, for the buttonbands.

Remember to work the buttonholes every 8 (9, 10, 10) garter stitch ridges of buttonbands.

Work SLIP STITCH PATTERN once.

SLIP STITCH PATTERN:

Row 1: (RS) With MC, knit.

Row 2: With MC, knit (makes one ridge).

Row 3: With MC, K5, with CC3, knit to last 5 sts, with MC, K5.

Row 4: With MC K5, with CC3, knit to last 5 sts, with MC K5 (makes one ridge).

Row 5: With MC, K5, with CC4, K1, with yarn in back SL1, *K3, with yarn in back SL1; repeat from * to last 6 stitches, K1; with MC, K5.

Row 6: With MC, K5, with CC4, K1, with yarn in front SL1, *K3, with yarn in front SL1; repeat from * to last 6 stitches, K1; with MC, K5.

Row 7: as Row 3.

Row 8: as Row 4 (makes one ridge).

Row 9: as Row 1.

Row 10: as Row 2 (makes a ridge).

Reminder: *Remember to work the buttonholes!*

Work BOBBLE PATTERN once.

BOBBLE PATTERN:

Row 1: (RS) With MC K5, with CC1, knit to last 5 sts, with MC K5.

Row 2: as Row 1 (makes a ridge).

Row 3: (RS) With MC K5, with CC1, purl to last 5 sts, with MC K5.

Row 4: as Row 1.

Row 5: as Row 3.

Row 6: as Row 3.

Row 7: (RS) With MC K5, with CC1 K1, with CC2 MB, *with CC1 K3, with CC2 MB; repeat from * to last 6 sts, with CC1 K1, with MC K5.

Row 8: as Row 3.

Row 9: (RS) as Row 3.

Row 10: as Row 1.

Row 11: as Row 3.

Row 12: as Row 1.

MB: Make Bobble: into next stitch K1, yo, K1, yo, K1 (5 sts), Turn. P2tog, P1, P2tog, Turn. Slip 2 sts together knitwise, K1, Pass 2 slipped sts over end of needle.

Repeat Slip Stitch Pattern followed by the Bobble Pattern 0 (1, 1, 2) more time(s).

Work Slip Stitch Pattern once more.

Reality Check:
Pattern repeats for the Body of the Sweater:
Size 1:
  Slip Stitch Pattern/Bobble Pattern/ Slip Stitch Pattern.

Sizes 2 & 4:
  Slip Stitch Pattern/Bobble Pattern/ Slip Stitch Pattern/Bobble Pattern/ Slip Stitch Pattern.

Size 6:
  Slip Stitch Pattern/Bobble Pattern/ Slip Stitch Pattern/Bobble Pattern/ Slip Stitch Pattern/Bobble Pattern/ Slip Stitch Pattern.

BORDER

Next Row: With MC, knit.

Next Row: K5, purl to last 5 stitches, K5.

Knit every row in MC until 5 ridges show on RS, ending after a WS row.

Continue knitting every row, if necessary, until sweater measures 12 (13, 15, 17)"/30.5 (33, 38, 43) cm, ending after a WS row. You can lengthen the sweater here and work to desired length.

With WS facing, **Cast Off** knitways.

FINISHING

Sew sleeve seams if necessary, closing gap at underarm.

Weave in ends.

Sew buttons over the buttonholes on the Left Band for girls or Right Band for boys.

Block if necessary.

TECHNICAL BITS

EQUIPMENT

As any good craftsperson knows, you need good tools to do your job right. Luckily, for this craft you don't need to run out and buy a circular saw for a couple hundred dollars! However, you should have a good range of knitting needles appropriate for the job.

You'll need:

- Circular needles;
- Sets of double-pointed needles; and
- A cable needle, if you are doing a cable design
- markers;
- Tapestry needle or blunt sewing-up needle.

CIRCULAR NEEDLES

Circular needles come in many varieties. You can get them in plastic, steel, nickel and bamboo as a minimum. Plastic and bamboo needles are good if you are working with a slippery yarn (cotton, some wools, mohair etc), and they are also light and warm. Metal needles are great for speed as they slide your yarn along with no hesitation. Try out different needles with different yarn to see what you like.

Circular needles also come in varying lengths. Commonly they are:

> 40 cm / 16 inches
> 60 cm / 24 inches
> 80 cm / 36 inches
> 100 cm / 40 inches

For the designs in this book, you only need the 16"/40 cm and the 24"/60 cm lengths.

It is important to carefully check the join where the needle tips are attached to the connecting plastic wire. If the join is rough you will be unhappy working with these needles because they may catch or snag your yarn as you move it back and forth across the join.

When you get new circular needles they will be coiled up in the package. If you try to work with the needles without preparing them first they will, at the very least, be stiff and hard to work with. At their worst, they'll try to coil up your knitting as you work on it, and drive you crazy.

To prepare your needles for comfortable knitting, remove them from the package and place them in really hot tap water. The plastic connecting wire should relax quite a bit and become pliable and relatively straight. Do not store the needle back in the package when finished with it.

DOUBLE-POINTED NEEDLES

You will need these for the sleeves worked in the round, and small items like hats or socks.

Double-pointed needles (dpns) are available in sets of four or five needles. We always use five needle sets but this is a matter of personal preference. Whatever number of needles you use, one needle is used to work the stitches while the knit stitches rest on the other needles.

As with circular needles, double-pointed needles come in various materials such as wood, bamboo, plastic and various metals. They also come in a range of lengths, from glove sizes which are less than 5 inches, to short needles around 5½ to 6 inches (14 cm to 15 cm), to common lengths of 7-ish inches to 20 inches (18 cm to 51 cm).

The short needles are quite useful for socks and small items such as children's clothing.

PATTERN SIZING

When we did the research for the book, we were astounded at the range of sizes for kids. What to do? Rather than having each designer come up with their own sizes we decided to create a uniform set of sizes for all the patterns. There may be minor differences in size to accommodate a stitch or colour pattern but otherwise they're pretty much the same.

All the sizes have a finished measurement and you're best to check this measurement against the size of the small one you are knitting for.

You can measure a garment they own that fits well, in a similar weight of yarn, and check against our measurements in order to select the right size.

If in doubt, a larger size is better to grow into than a smaller size which may fit for only a week!

Gauge Swatch

We do recommend working a gauge swatch. A swatch gives you a sample of your knitting with a particular yarn and needle size.

Work the Swatch:

If you are going to be knitting one of the pullover patterns, then you should knit your swatch in the round. Adjust the needle as you work until you find the right needle size to obtain the given tension.

If you are going to be knitting one of the cardigans, then do your swatch flat, knitting on the right side and purling on the wrong side.

With a ruler, count the number of stitches you have over 4"/10 cm of knitting.

If you are getting too few stitches over 4"/10 cm then try a smaller needle size. If you are getting more stitches in the 4"/10 cm than the gauge calls for, then try a larger needle.

You should also treat the swatch to whatever washing method you will be using for the finished garment. If the yarn is a machine washable (superwash) yarn then machine wash the swatch and measure it after it's dry. If it's a hand wash item, take it to the sink and wash by hand for your test.

How to Make an I-cord

Elizabeth Zimmermann, an innovative knitter, teacher and writer of the knitting world named this the idiot cord, now known as I-cord. It is a knit cord used for attaching children's mittens together, for finishing edging techniques, to begin or end the top of hats and for decorative details on knitted items.

Cast On 4 stitches onto a double-point needle.

The stitches have been pushed to the other end of the double-pointed needle and the right-hand needle is inserted to knit the first stitch of the "knit 4 stitches".

*Slide the 4 stitches to the other end of the needle. **DO NOT TURN.**

Knit 4 stitches [on the first stitch pull wool from the last stitch up to the first stitch and knit tightly]; repeat from * to desired length.

3-Needle Cast Off

With stitches for body on 1 needle and stitches of the skirt on another needle, hold both needles together (with body on back needle and skirt on front needle, wrong sides facing to make a ridged seam). Working on the right side of the sweater, with another (3rd) needle of working size, beginning at the outer edge:

1. Insert 3rd needle into first stitch on front left needle and without removing it, insert 3rd needle into first stitch on back needle and knit these two stitches together.

2. Repeat once more.

3. There are 2 stitches on right needle; pass first stitch over second stitch and off end of needle (the same as a regular Cast Off).

Repeat 1 & 3 until all the stitches are Cast Off.

FINISHING

TASSELS

Tassels are made by wrapping yarn around a piece of cardboard 3-4"/8-10 cm wide and about 3"/7.5 cm long. Wrap the yarn around the cardboard until it is sufficiently thick - 25 to 30 times - and break the yarn. Thread more yarn through a sewing-up needle and use this to wrap yarn around the top of the yarn on the cardboard a few times then tie a knot tightly. Break the yarn. Slide scissors between the cardboard and the wrapped yarn, at the opposite end of the knot, and cut through the wrapped yarn. Then, tightly wrap another strand of yarn about an inch/2.5 cm down from the knotted end to secure the tassel. Trim the tassel to even the ends if necessary.

SEWING ON BUTTONS

For extra security we suggest the use of shirt buttons sewn on the back of the actual sweater button.

Set a button over the buttonhole on the appropriate side. Using button thread, close the hole as you attach the button. After 2-3 passes of the thread, attach a small shirt button on the wrong side of the buttonband and sew through both buttons. This adds stability and strength for the buttons.

* * * * * * * * * *

OTHER READING

Whether you are a absolute or relative beginner, or an experienced knitter there are always useful and interesting books and reference materials that are worthwhile to look through.

For knitting Top Down:
Knitting from the Top by Barbara G. Walker

Reference books:
Knitting for Dummies by Pam Allen, Hungry Minds, 2002. This is an excellent reference book.

The Complete Idiot's Guide to Knitting and Crocheting by Gail Diven and Cindy Kitchel, Alpha Books, 1999.

The Vogue Reference Book, Pantheon, 1989.

The Principles of Knitting, Methods and Techniques of Hand Knitting by June Hemmons Hiatt, Simon and Schuster, 1988.

For knitting in the round:
Any book by Elizabeth Zimmermann! All of these books are published by Schoolhouse Press and can be obtained from the web site: http://www.school-housepress.com

Knitting Around, Knitting Without Tears, Knitter's Almanac, Knitting Workshop. All are excellent!

The Sweater Workshop by Jacqueline Fee, Down East Books, 2002.

Knitting Ganseys by Beth Brown-Reinsel, Interweave Press, 1993.

SUPPLY SOURCES

S. R. Kertzer
50 Trowers Rd, Woodbridge, ON, L4L 7K6, Canada
In the US: PMB 192, 60 Industrial Parkway, Cheektowaga, NY, 14227
(800) 263-2354, Fax: (905) 856-5585
http://www.kertzer.com
(Naturally yarns, Butterfly cotton, Stylecraft & Emu)

Shelridge Farm
R.R. #2, Ariss, ON, N0B 1B0, Canada
(519) 846-9662, Fax: (519) 846-0250
http://www.shelridge.com

Classic Elite Yarns, Inc.
12 Perkins St., Lowell, MA 01854

Knitting Software: www.software4knitting.com. The Stitch and Motif Maker V3.0 was used to create the charts used in this book.

Cabin Fever
Our patterns and books are available wholesale or retail.
We have a number of other top down patterns and many, many, knit in the round garments for adults and children which you can find at good yarn shops or visit our web site at:
http://www.cabinfever.ca
(800) 671-9112

INDEX

3-Needle Cast Off 102
Abbreviations 13
Ball band 13
Bind-off 14
Circular knitting. See Knitting in the round.
Circular needles 101
Decreasing
    knitting two stitches together 14
    purling two stitches together 14
    slip, slip, knit 15
Double-point needles 101
Dye lot 14
Equipment 101
Finishing 103
Gauge
    circular knitting 14, 102
    flat knitting 14, 102
I-cord (idiot cord) 102
Increasing
    adding a single stitch 16
    make one increase 16
    yarn overs. See yarn over.
Joining first circular stitch 10
Joining in the round 10
k2tog (knit two stitches together) 14
Knitting language 13
Knitting
    circular 8
    flat 8
    from the top down 8
    in the round 8
    in one piece 8
    tools. See equipment.

Knitting in the round. See circular knitting.
Knitting markers. See stitch markers.
Knitting needles 101
Knitting supplies. See tools.
Label on yarn. See ball band.
m1 (make one increase) 16
Markers. See stitch marker.
p2tog (purl two stitches together) 14
phrases in knitting patterns. See knitting language.
Sizes of needles 101
Stitch gauge. See gauge.
Stitch markers 15
Stitches
    Garter Stitch 14
    Stocking Stitch 15
    Twisted 10
Supplies. See equipment
Swatches 102
Tassels 103
Tension gauge 14, 102
Top down. See knitting from the top down.
Twisted stitches. See joining in the round.
Yarn markers. See stitch markers.
Yarn over 16
yo. See yarn over.